The Wisdom *of*

John Paul II

Nick Bakalar is a New York writer and the author of ten other books on a variety of subjects.

Richard Balkin is a literary agent, packager, and freelance writer in Amherst, Massachusetts.

Father John White is a priest of the Roman Catholic Diocese of Rockville Centre, New York.

ALSO AVAILABLE

The Book of Job
The Confessions of St. Augustine
The Desert Fathers
Devotions upon Emergent Occasions
The Imitation of Christ
The Little Flowers of St. Francis of Assisi
The Rule of St. Benedict
John Henry Newman: Selected Sermons, Prayers, and Devotions
The Bhagavad Gita
The Spiritual Exercises of St. Ignatius
The Five Scrolls
Buddhist Wisdom

The Wisdom *of* John Paul II

The Pope on Life's Most Vital Questions

COMPILED BY

Nick Bakalar and Richard Balkin

INTRODUCTION BY

Father John White

VINTAGE SPIRITUAL CLASSICS

VINTAGE BOOKS

A DIVISION OF RANDOM HOUSE, INC.

NEW YORK

FIRST VINTAGE SPIRITUAL CLASSICS EDITION, NOVEMBER 2001

Library of Congress Cataloging-in-Publication Data
John Paul II, Pope, 1920–
[Wisdom of John Paul II]
The wisdom of Pope John Paul II : the Pope on life's most vital questions / compiled by
Nick Bakalar and Richard Balkin ; introduction by John White.
p. cm.
Originally published: The wisdom of John Paul II. San Francisco : HarperSanFrancisco,
©1995.
Includes bibliographical references.
ISBN 0-375-72732-9
1. Spiritual life—Catholic Church. 2. Church and the world. 3. Catholic Church—
Doctrines. 4. Conduct of life. I. Bakalar, Nick. II. Balkin, Richard. III. Title.

BX2350.2 .J638 2001

282—dc21   2001025859

Book design by Fritz Metsch

www.vintagebooks.com

Printed in the United States of America

3   5   7   9   10   8   6   4

To Tony and Anne

Sine amicitia vitam esse nullam.

O Divine Master, Grant that I may not so much seek to be consoled as to console, to be understood as to understand, to be loved as to love; for it is in giving that we receive, it is in pardoning that we are pardoned, and it is in dying that we are born to eternal life.

—PRAYER OF ST. FRANCIS OF ASSISI
Speech to Interreligious Leaders at Los Angeles,
September 16, 1987

CONTENTS

ACKNOWLEDGMENTS

The editors would like to thank Christopher Lee, Thomas Kelly, and especially Anna Bonta for their research assistance. We were particularly fortunate in having Father John White as an adviser on theological points in the manuscript, as the author of a superb introduction to this volume, and, most important, as a friend. We acknowledge the publishing contribution of St. Paul Books and Media, which publishes all the encyclicals, apostolic letters, and other documents of the Vatican and Pope John Paul II at very reasonable prices. We also indebted to Father Jude of St. Hyacinth Seminary, Beverly Wilson of the St. Hyacinth Seminary Library, and Sister Regina Melican of St. Joseph's Seminary Library for their assistance in gathering material. And we owe a particular debt of gratitude to the Libreria Editrice Vaticana for allowing us to reprint the Pope's words. Dawn Davis of Vintage Books was instrumental in helping us put together this Revised Edition.

INTRODUCTION

On October 16, 1978, Karol Józef Wojtyla of Kracόw, Poland, was elected His Holiness, Pope John Paul II, leader of the world's 1 billion Roman Catholics, the 262nd successor of St. Peter, and the first non-Italian Pope in 455 years. The newly elected Pope's compatriot and close friend, Cardinal Stefan Wyszynski from Warsaw, is reported to have said to him: "If God has chosen you, God has chosen you to lead the Church into the third millennium." Later today, January 6, 2001, the Feast of the Epiphany, the Pope will close the Holy Door in St. Peter's Basilica, symbolizing the end of the Church's Great Jubilee Year celebration of the bimillennium of the birth of Christ. When the Pope kneels in prayer before the giant closed door in the vestibule of St. Peter's, how stunningly prophetic the words of Cardinal Wyszynski will be shown to have been! Only when historians review the Church's Great Jubilee Year program, the exhaustive preparations, the astonishing worldwide calendar of events and activities, the apostolic letters, exhortations, and papal sermons, and the overall influence of this commemoration upon his Papacy and the entire papal program of John Paul II will it become clear how deeply did this prophecy of his trusted mentor enter the soul of the Pope.

From the very beginning of his pontificate twenty-two years ago, the approaching turn of the millennium has never been far from the mind of the Pope. Just how central the milestone of the year 2000 and its spiritual significance and potential for a renewed Christianity have been to the Pope's thinking and teaching can best be discovered in his apostolic letter titled *Tertio Millennio Adveniente* (Toward the Third Millennium), issued in November 1994. In that seminal document, which announced the formal commencement of the Church's preparations for the Jubilee, John

Paul reveals that "preparing for the year 2000" should be understood to be the essential "key of my Pontificate." This is to say that the wealth of more than twenty years of papal teachings, his staggering travel log, the synods of bishops, commemorations of major historical and religious events, must all be seen theologically, as components of a larger providential plan for a revivified Christianity in the third millennium, the marks of which are a deeper devotion to the person of Jesus Christ and a more generous commitment to daily living of his gospel of love. Indeed, so total is the claim made by Jubilee 2000 upon the Pope's understanding of his own mission, and his overall theological perspective, that even the premier and central religious and spiritual event of the century for the Pope, Vatican Council II (1962–1965), is to be understood as preparation, the most important of all preparations in God's plan, for the third Christian millennium.

The Pope went on to say in *Tertio Millennio Adveniente* that all of the Church's planning and preparation would be shaped by the spirit of the Vatican Council and "expressed in a renewed commitment to apply as faithfully as possible, the teaching of Vatican II," which gave to the sons and daughters of the Church new encouragement and support for discovering God in their lives, and for using their gifts for the good of their neighbors and communities, and, through a commitment to social justice, the whole world. The Pope then offered a novel analogy that reveals the papal mind concerning the relationship between the Council and the millennium: As the season of Advent is to Christmas, so the Vatican Council is to the Church's celebration of the Jubilee Year. That is, in some ways, an extraordinary linkage. No wonder, then, that when the Public Broadcasting System recently presented an in-depth profile and analysis of the pontificate of John Paul II, the producers chose to title it *John Paul II: The Millennial Pope.* Beyond a doubt, the producers got it right.

By any measure, Pope John Paul's program for the Great Jubilee 2000, now completed, must be judged a dramatic success. His collaboration with the world's Catholic bishops and the national conferences of bishops in shaping a Jubilee Year consciousness among the Catholic people, creating an awareness of the uniqueness and opportunity of the moment, engaging it through special prayers, liturgical celebrations, community outreach, and justice and peace activities, by all accounts appears to have exceeded even the Vatican's expectations. All Jubilee Year celebrations, which occur every fifty years throughout the Church's history, are especially devoted to a proclamation of the mercy of God, the forgiveness of sins, and the need for reconciliation between individuals. Throughout the Great Jubilee of the Year 2000, all across the world, diocesan-wide "Days of Reconciliation" were held following extensive advertising and educational campaigns, inviting all Catholics, but especially those who had been away from the Church, to "come home" and to experience the mercy of God. These special days centered on an all-day availability of the sacrament of reconciliation. By all reports these efforts were very successful, particularly here in the United States.

A range of papal projects and activities designed to call particular attention to different segments of the community with special needs, such as the elderly, the sick, the poor; to injustices and inequities around the world, especially the crushing burden of debt upon the world's poor nations; and to the need for forgiveness and reconciliation between and among people were widely covered by the media. The "Homily of the Holy Father Asking Pardon," delivered on the First Sunday of Lent, March 12, 2000, asking forgiveness for offenses committed throughout history by "some sons and daughters of the Church," particularly those offenses directed against the Church's "older brothers and sisters in the faith," as the Pope has in the past referred to the Jewish people, and especially for Christian silence in the face of the monstrous evil perpetrated by the Holocaust, became the occasion and inspiration for widespread Catholic soul-searching and reflection. The papal pilgrimage to the Holy Land and visit to Israel in March, which included the Pope's prayer for forgiveness and reconciliation at Jerusalem's Wailing Wall, was a poignant event chronicled around the world. The World Youth Day event in Rome in August attracted some 2 million young participants from every corner of the globe and generated enormous attention to the Jubilee Year and outpouring for the Pope, particularly across Europe and Asia. Special celebrations for the sick, the elderly, immigrants, and prisoners were exquisitely presented, pointed and inspiring.

Some mention should be made of Pope John Paul's Jubilee

Year effort to invite the wealthy nations of the world to forgive Third World debt and to join the growing movement for a comprehensive plan for global debt relief. At the heart of all Jubilee Year celebrations in the Church's history is the theme of the forgiveness of debt, which has always included economic and interpersonal as well as spiritual considerations. The jubilee principle guiding the Christian's response to indebtedness is fundamental: As God forgives each of us our debts, so must we forgive those indebted to us. And this forgiveness, in jubilee spirituality, should be very real and practical. The Pope made the global debt relief initiative a central campaign of Jubilee Year 2000. Supported by the rock star Bono of the Irish band U2, along with a coalition of religious, governmental, and secular leaders from around the world, the Pope led the successful effort to convince the Congress of the United States to allot $435 million to the United States' share of the global relief initiative and succeeded in moving this issue to the World Bank and the International Monetary Fund, as well as front and center at the United Nations and before the conscience of the world. From the perspective of Catholic social teaching, this is a most welcome and positive development. The Pope believes this to be a most important event born out of his Jubilee Year efforts.

Today, January 6, 2001, on the Feast of the Epiphany, the Great Jubilee Year celebration of the birth of Christ two thousand years ago in Bethlehem, "the greatest event in history," as the Pope has put it, comes to an end. Pope John Paul has lived to see the Church and the world cross over this threshold of history. Is the era of John Paul II, the Millennial Pope, also now completed? Is it possible that the Pope might shock the Church and become the first Pope since Clement V, 706 years ago, to retire from the papacy, as a leading German bishop recently suggested might happen? It is quite impossible to know the answer to those questions, at least for now. But the frail, weary Pope, eighty years old, suffering from Parkinson's disease and a bad hip, has survived the brutal, frenetic Jubilee Year calendar. *The New York Times* reported on January 2, 2001, that the Pope looked better and healthier than he has in a while as he delivered the World Day of Prayer for Peace Message on New Year's Day at St. Peter's. Who can know the mind of God in this matter? What we do know about the Pope is this: The man who was heralded by *Time* magazine as one of the twenty people of the twentieth century who "helped define the political and social fabric of our times," who has been called by some "the person of the century" and by others "the prophet of the millennium," Pope John Paul continues to push ahead with his plan for his Papacy, the Church, and the cause of freedom, peace, and justice in the world.

And despite his physical limitations and infirmities, the Pope continues to provoke and command, sometimes more strenuously than ever. He is still unafraid to set out before the world his understanding of the meaning of human life and his vision for a better world. By his astounding determination and persistence in carrying out his mission for the soul of humanity and the salvation of this world, he continues to compel massive attention and enormous respect. His more than one hundred trips throughout the world to awaken faith, stir compassion, and console the anxious have touched the soul of an entire generation of humanity. As leader of the Church's crusade for the poor nations of the world, the Pope has campaigned with the rock star Bono and presided over a Woodstock-like prayer festival for young people in Bologna, where he hummed and tapped to Bob Dylan singing "Knocking on Heaven's Door." The fierce critic of Western culture, with its hype, conspicuous consumption, and preoccupation with celebrity, is quite possibly the biggest celebrity ever. He is old in years but young at heart; conservative and liberal; a traditionalist and a progressive; a reactionary and a radical. He is, as it has been put, a sign of contradiction, offering a witness the likes of which has never before been seen.

The Pope continues to have many critics, both inside and outside the Church. Some argue that while encouraging dissent against authoritarian regimes, he himself has squashed not only dissent but even discussion of positions contrary to his own. Critics insist that he has proven unreasonable over the issues of women's ordination and a married clergy. He is routinely condemned for what is said to be a preoccupation with abortion and sexual ethics. Some of the harshest criticism of all stems from his policy of appointing very conservative bishops, theologically and politically, from outside dioceses, and, more often than not, disregarding the advice of local church leaders.

Despite the criticism, and the acclaim, the Pope has held to his vision unwaveringly, absorbed both the condemnation and the applause, and given his best in the service of his mission. He continues to do so.

This book represents a broad overview of Pope John Paul's thinking, vision, and hopes at this extraordinary moment in the history of the Church and the world. The book is divided into subject categories that grow out of the body of John Paul's teachings, sermons, and writings, with an editorial headnote introducing each section. The editors offer a representative sample of passages in the hope of capturing the heart, mind, spirit, and soul of the Pope in his own words.

Epiphany is a Greek word that in English best translates as "manifestation." The Feast of the Epiphany celebrates the first manifestation of the Lord to the Gentiles, symbolized in the coming of the Magi to Bethlehem to pay homage to the Christ child. One of the many manifestations God is certainly offering the people of our time on this Feast of the Epiphany, 2001, is that in the person of the Holy Father, Pope John Paul II, God is visiting His people, with a message of love and hope, solidarity and peace; with an invitation to faith and prayer, integrity and holiness. It is my prayer today that this book will help to make that manifestation brighter and clearer.

It is a special grace to complete this brief introduction to the words of this most important, faithful, and inspiring servant of God, Pope John Paul II, on the closing day of the Great Jubilee Year celebration of the bimillennium of the birth of the Prince of Peace and the gospel of love.

FATHER JOHN WHITE
New York
January 6, 2001

The Pope's encyclicals and the apostolic exhortations and letters are cited by name and year. The *Ad Limina* addresses, which always occur in Rome, are identified by date and by the group of bishops to whom the Pope is speaking. Most of these quotations, however, come from the occasional speeches the Pope gives all over the world. These are cited by date and place and, where it seemed pertinent to the subject, by the audience as well: workers for speeches on work, youth groups for speeches about young people, the United Nations for certain remarks on human rights, and so on. In addition, where it seemed helpful, we have cited the subject or title of the speech as it appeared in its written form. Many of the Pope's speeches are presented to general audiences in the Vatican, large crowds at sports stadiums, smaller groups at airports, and so on. These speeches are cited by place and date only.

The Wisdom *of*
John Paul II

Pope John Paul calls on Christians to renew their spiritual lives. The Pope insists that just as the body needs earthly food for growth, the soul needs to drink from the living waters of the Gospel. Only through tending to both physical and spiritual needs can a person lead a fully integrated life.

John Paul recognizes the value of the awakening of the religious sense in contemporary spiritual movements. These movements, for example, urge a deeper respect for the earth and transcend merely rational forms of religion. They awaken the imagination and religious sensibilities that have been buried under modern materialism and secularization. But the Pope also clearly rejects modern forms of spirituality that conflict with the Gospel message and confuse rather than clarify the human being's relationship to God.

John Paul emphasizes in particular the centrality of the sacraments of the Eucharist and penance. Christians witness God's love for humankind in the eucharistic meal and receive God's mercy in the sacrament of penance. Through participation in the sacraments, Christians today deepen their spiritual journeys.

In the race for technological progress, human beings have become estranged from themselves. As a result, they turn to new spiritual movements that attempt to bridge this chasm. Although John Paul believes that the Church can learn from contemporary movements in spirituality, he holds firmly to the past two thousand years of Christian tradition. Christians in the modern world face the challenge of meeting new, complex needs while at the same time holding fast to their Biblical heritage.

CONTEMPORARY SPIRITUALITY

When individuals and communities do not see a rigorous respect for the moral, cultural and spiritual requirements, based on the dignity of the person and on the proper identity of each community, beginning with the family and religious societies, then all the rest—availability of goods, abundance of technical resources applied to daily life, a certain level of material well-being—will prove unsatisfying and in the end contemptible.

ENCYCLICAL: ON SOCIAL CONCERNS (*Sollicitudo Rei Socialis*), 1987

Development which is merely economic is incapable of setting man free; on the contrary, it will end by enslaving him further. Development that does not include the *cultural, transcendent and religious dimensions* of man and society, to the extent that it does not recognize the existence of such dimensions and does not endeavor to direct its goals and priorities toward the same, is *even less* conducive to authentic liberation. Human beings are totally free only when they are completely *themselves,* in the fullness of their rights and duties. The same can be said about society as a whole.

ENCYCLICAL: ON SOCIAL CONCERNS (*Sollicitudo Rei Socialis*), 1987

The increasing religious indifference leads to the loss of the sense of God and of His holiness, which, in turn, is translated into a loss of a sense of the sacred, of mystery and of the capacity for wonder. These are human dispositions which predispose a person to dialogue and to an encounter with God. Such indifference almost inevitably leads to a false moral autonomy and a secularistic lifestyle which excludes God. The loss of the sense of God is followed by a loss of the sense of sin, which has its roots in the moral conscience of the individual. This is a great obstacle to conversion.

Lineamenta FOR THE ASSEMBLY OF THE SYNOD OF BISHOPS FOR AMERICA, September 18, 1996

In a world pervaded by audiovisual messages of every kind, it is necessary to recover areas of silence which allow God to make

His voice heard, and the soul to understand and welcome it. This is what we are taught by the shining example of countless saints and blesseds who have preceded us, glorifying God with the prayerful recollection of their life, and of martyrs, who for love chose "the silence" of the total gift of their life as a response to God's love perceived in the Word and in the Eucharist.

ADDRESS TO THE CONGREGATION FOR DIVINE WORSHIP,
May 3, 1996

Many people today are puzzled and ask: What is the point of the consecrated life? Why embrace this kind of life when there are so many unmet needs in the areas of charity and of evangelization itself to which one can respond even without assuming the particular commitments of the consecrated life? Is the consecrated life not a kind of "waste" of human energies which might be used more efficiently for a greater good, for the benefit of humanity and the church? . . . What in people's eyes can seem a waste is, for the individuals captivated in the depths of their heart by the beauty and goodness of the Lord, an obvious response of love, a joyful expression of gratitude for having been admitted in a unique way to the knowledge of the Son and to a sharing in His divine mission in the world.

EXHORTATION ON THE CONSECRATED LIFE, March 25, 1996

Lent is thus a providential opportunity for fostering the spiritual detachment from riches necessary if we are to open ourselves to God. As Christians, we must direct our entire lives to Him, for we know that in this world we have no fixed abode: "our commonwealth is in heaven" (Phil 3:20). At the end of Lent, the celebration of the Paschal Mystery shows how the Lenten journey of purification culminates in the free and loving gift of self to the Father. It is by taking this path that Christ's disciples learn how to rise above themselves and their selfish interests in order to encounter in love their brothers and sisters.

MESSAGE FOR LENT 1996

It is helpful to recall that a modern state cannot make atheism or religion one of its political ordinances. The state, while distancing itself from all extremes of fanaticism or secularism, should encourage a harmonious social climate and a suitable legislation which enables every person and every religious confession to live their faith freely, to express that faith in the context of public life and to count on adequate resources and opportunities to bring its spiritual, moral and civic benefits to bear on the life of the nation.

THE DOCTRINE OF FREEDOM AND SOLIDARITY
Homily at the Mass in Havana's Revolution Plaza, January 25, 1998

American Catholics, in common with other Christians and all believers, have a responsibility to ensure that the mystery of God and the truth about humanity that is revealed in the mystery of God are not banished from public life.

MORAL TRUTH, CONSCIENCE AND AMERICAN DEMOCRACY
Ad Limina Address to U.S. Bishops, June 27, 1998

The disciple of Christ is constantly challenged by a spreading "practical atheism"—an indifference to God's loving plan which obscures the religious and moral sense of the human heart. Many either think and act as if God did not exist, or tend to "privatize" religious belief and practice, so that there exists a bias toward indifferentism and the elimination of any real reference to binding truths and moral values. When the basic principles which inspire and direct human behavior are fragmentary and even at times contradictory, society increasingly struggles to maintain harmony and a sense of its own destiny. In a desire to find some common ground on which to build its programs and policies, it tends to restrict the contribution of those whose moral conscience is formed by their religious beliefs.

Ad Limina ADDRESS TO BISHOPS FROM NEW JERSEY
AND PENNSYLVANIA, November 11, 1993

The Church feels the duty to proclaim the liberation of millions of human beings, the duty to help this liberation become firmly established (cf. *EN,* 30); but she also feels the corresponding duty to proclaim liberation in its integral and profound meanings, as Jesus proclaimed and realized it (cf. *EN,* 9). Liberation made up of reconciliation and forgiveness. Liberation springing from the reality of being children of God, whom we are able to call Abba, Father (Rom 8:15), a reality which makes us recognize in every man a brother of ours, capable of being transformed in his heart through God's mercy. Liberation that, with the energy of love, urges us toward fellowship, the summit and fullness of which we find in the Lord. Liberation as the overcoming of the various forms of slavery and man-made idols, and as the growth of the new man. Liberation that in the framework of the Church's proper mission is not reduced to the simple and narrow economic, political, social or cultural dimension, and is not sacrificed to the demands of any strategy, practice or short-term solution (cf. *EN*, 33).

ADDRESS TO LATIN AMERICAN BISHOPS AT PUEBLA,
February 8, 1979

It is not an exaggeration to say that man's relationship to God and the demand for a religious "experience" are the crux of a profound crisis affecting the human spirit. While the secularization of many aspects of life continues, there is a new quest for "spirituality" as evidenced in the appearance of many religious and healing movements which look to respond to the crisis of values in Western society. This stirring of the *homo religiosus* produces some positive and constructive results, such as the search for new meaning in life, a new ecological sensitivity and the desire to go beyond a cold, rationalistic religiosity. On the other hand, this religious reawakening includes some very ambiguous elements which are incompatible with the Christian faith.

BEYOND NEW AGE IDEAS: SPIRITUAL RENEWAL
Ad Limina Address to U.S. Bishops, May 28, 1993

Modern rationalism does not tolerate mystery. It does not accept the mystery of man as male and female nor is it willing to admit that the full truth about man has been revealed in Jesus Christ. In particular, it does not accept the great mystery proclaimed in the Letter to the Ephesians, but radically opposes it. It may well acknowledge, in the context of a vague deism, the possibility and even the need for a supreme or divine being, but it firmly rejects the idea of a God who became man in order to save man. For rationalism it is unthinkable that God should be the redeemer, much less that He should be the bridegroom, the primordial and unique source of the human love between spouses. Rationalism provides a radically different way of looking at creation and the meaning of human existence. But once man begins to lose sight of a God who loves him, a God who calls man through Christ to live in Him and with Him, and once the family no longer has the possibility of sharing in the great mystery, what is left except the mere temporal dimension of life? Earthly life becomes nothing more than the scenario of a battle for existence, of a desperate search for gain, and financial gain before all else.

LETTER TO FAMILIES FOR THE INTERNATIONAL YEAR OF THE
FAMILY, February 22, 1994

To many people, mercy and conversion may seem like poor tools for solving social problems. Some are tempted to accept ideologies that use force to carry out their programs and impose their vision. Such means sometimes produce what appear to be successes. But these successes are not real. Force and manipulation have nothing to do with true human development and the defense of human dignity. Catholic social teaching is totally different, not only as regards goals, but also as regards the means to be used. For the Christian, putting right human ills must necessarily take into account the reality of creation and redemption. It means treating every human being as a unique child of God, a brother or sister of Jesus Christ. The path of human solidarity is the path of service; and true service means selfless love, open to the needs of all, without distinction of persons, with the explicit purpose of reinforcing each person's sense of God-given dignity.

ADDRESS TO CATHOLIC CHARITIES, CALIFORNIA,
September 13, 1987

Every age poses new challenges and new temptations for the People of God on their pilgrimage, and our own is no exception. We face a growing secularism that tries to exclude God and religious truth from human affairs. We face an insidious relativism that undermines the absolute truth of Christ and the truths of faith, and tempts believers to think of them as merely one set of beliefs or opinions among others. We face a materialistic consumerism that offers superficially attractive but empty promises conferring material comfort at the price of inner emptiness. We face an alluring hedonism that offers a whole series of pleasures that will

never satisfy the human heart. All these attitudes can influence our sense of good and evil at the very moment when social and scientific progress requires strong ethical guidance. Once alienated from Christian faith and practice by these and other deceptions, people often commit themselves to passing fads, or to bizarre beliefs that are either shallow or fanatical.

ADDRESS TO LAITY, ST. MARY'S CATHEDRAL, SAN FRANCISCO,
September 18, 1987

A few years ago, there was much talk of the secularized world, the post-Christian era. Fashion changes, but a profound reality remains. Christians today must be formed to live in a world which largely ignores God or which, in religious matters, in place of an exacting and fraternal dialogue, stimulating for all, too often founders in a debasing indifferentism, if it does not remain in a scornful attitude of "suspicion" in the name of the progress it has made in the field of scientific "explanations." To "hold on" in this world, to offer to all a "dialogue of salvation" in which each person feels respected in his or her most basic dignity, the dignity of one who is seeking God, we need a catechesis which trains the young people and adults of our communities to remain clear and consistent in their faith, to affirm serenely their Christian and Catholic identity, to "see Him who is invisible" and to adhere so firmly to the absoluteness of God that they can be witnesses to Him in a materialistic civilization that denies Him.

CATECHESIS IN OUR TIME, October 1979

In his world travels, Pope John Paul has taken a very direct approach to governments that do not live up to basic standards of human rights. He visited Buenos Aires, where he referred directly to the Argentine government's "dirty war" and pointedly held a meeting with one of the few bishops in the country who had spoken out against the government. In Africa, in 1985, he made a direct appeal to President Mobutu of Zaire and condemned South Africa's apartheid. In South Korea, he spoke both publicly and privately with the president about the need for greater democracy and greater respect for personal liberty. No government is spared: The Holy Father has condemned equally governments of the left and the right for what he perceives as violations of human rights.

There is little question that the Pope's urgings have had practical effect. Mikhail Gorbachev gave the Holy Father much credit for the liberalization of Eastern Europe, and Lech Walesa acknowledged the Pope's aid as essential in preserving the gains of Solidarity in Poland.

Pope John Paul's campaign for human rights has always emphasized that social justice cannot be accomplished through class hatred or violence. In poor countries around the world, he has reminded the wealthy that their security cannot be bought at the expense of violations of the rights of the poor, and that redistribution of land, under certain circumstances, is a proper response to exploitation. If John Paul is a traditionalist in theological matters, he has not hesitated to advocate radical solutions to social problems.

HUMAN RIGHTS

The Christian view is that human beings are to be valued for what they are, not for what they have. In loving the poor and serving those in whatever need, the Church seeks above all to respect and heal their human dignity. The aim of Christian solidarity and service is to defend and promote, in the name of Jesus Christ, the dignity and fundamental human rights of every person. The Church bears witness to the fact that this dignity cannot be destroyed, whatever the situation of poverty, scorn, rejection or powerlessness to which a human being has been reduced. She shows her solidarity with those who do not count in a society by which they are rejected spiritually and sometimes even physically.

ADDRESS AT SAN ANTONIO, September 13, 1987

The depressed rural world, the worker who, with his sweat, waters also his affliction, cannot wait any longer for full and effective recognition of his dignity, which is not inferior to that of any other social sector.

ADDRESS TO INDIANS AND PEASANTS AT CUILAPA, GUATEMALA,
January 29, 1979

And how can we fail to consider the violence against life done to millions of human beings, especially children, who are forced into poverty, malnutrition and hunger because of an unjust distribution of resources between peoples and between social classes? And what of the violence inherent not only in wars as such, but in the scandalous arms trade, which spawns the many armed conflicts which stain our world with blood? What of the spreading of death caused by reckless tampering with the world's ecological balance, by the criminal spread of drugs or by the promotion of certain kinds of sexual activity which, besides being morally unacceptable, also involve grave risks to life? It is impossible to catalog completely the vast array of threats to human life, so many are the forms, whether explicit or hidden, in which they appear today!

ENCYCLICAL: THE GOSPEL OF LIFE (*Evangelium Vitae*), 1994

For the same reason, I consider it my duty once again to assert these inviolable rights of the human being from his conception on behalf of all the embryos which are often subjected to freezing cryopreservation), in many cases becoming an object of sheer experimentation or worse, destined to programmed destruction backed by law. Likewise, I confirm that it is gravely illicit, because of the dignity of the human person and of his having been called to life, to use methods of procreation which the instruction *Donum Vitae* has defined as unacceptable to moral doctrine.

ADDRESS AT A SYMPOSIUM ON EVANGELISM, May 24, 1996

And what are we to say of increasing violence against women and against children of both sexes? Today this is one of the most widespread violations of human rights, and tragically it has even become a terror tactic: women taken hostage, children barbarously slaughtered. To this must be added the violence of forced prostitution and child pornography, and the exploitation of children in the workplace in conditions of veritable slavery. Practical steps are needed to try to stop the spread of these forms of violence. In particular, appropriate legal measures are needed at both the national and international levels.

JUSTICE AND PEACE GO HAND IN HAND
Message for World Day of Peace, 1998

I am happy to take note of your words confirming the importance that your government attaches, in its relations with countries around the world, to the promotion of human rights and particularly to the fundamental human right of religious freedom, which is the guarantee of every other human right.

THE CHALLENGE TO AMERICAN DEMOCRACY
Address to Mrs. Corinne "Lindy" Boggs, Ambassador of the United States of America, December 16, 1997

We call to mind you, the aboriginal and indigenous peoples of America, who have suffered so much these past five centuries at the hands of the greedy and violent, and who even today enjoy so little of the abundance our lands have produced. As we proclaim to you the Gospel of Jesus Christ, we pledge ourselves to honor your culture and to support you in preserving your heritage.

ENCOUNTER WITH JESUS: CONVERSIONS, COMMUNION
AND SOLIDARITY
Message of the Special Assembly for America of the Synod of Bishops,
December 9, 1997

We want to speak to you, our brothers and sisters of African heritage, whose ancestors came to America in bondage as slaves. The wounds of those terrible centuries of slavery still sting the soul. We pledge ourselves to continue to work with you so that you may enjoy your full dignity as children of God, and so that you may always feel welcome in our churches and communities of faith.

ENCOUNTER WITH JESUS: CONVERSIONS, COMMUNION
AND SOLIDARITY
Message of the Special Assembly for America of the Synod of Bishops,
December 9, 1997

This same concern must be shown to the elderly, who are often neglected and left to fend for themselves. They must be respected as persons; it is important to care for them and to help them in ways which will promote their rights and ensure their greatest possible physical and spiritual well-being. The elderly must be protected from situations or pressures which could drive them to suicide; in particular they must be helped nowadays to resist the temptation of assisted suicide and euthanasia.

ECCLESIA IN AMERICA
Post-synodal Apostolic Exhortation, January 22, 1999

If the Church in America . . . intends to walk the path of solidarity, she must devote special attention to those ethnic groups which even today experience discrimination. Every attempt to marginalize the indigenous peoples must be eliminated. This means, first of all, respecting their territories and the pacts made with them; likewise, efforts must be made to satisfy their legitimate social, health and cultural requirements. And how can we overlook the need for reconciliation between the indigenous peoples and the societies in which they are living?

ECCLESIA IN AMERICA
Post-synodal Apostolic Exhortation, January 22, 1999

Nowadays, in America as elsewhere in the world, a model of society appears to be emerging in which the powerful predominate, setting aside and even eliminating the powerless: I am thinking here of unborn children, helpless victims of abortion; the elderly and incurably ill, subjected at times to euthanasia; and the many other people relegated to the margins of society by consumerism and materialism. Nor can I fail to mention the unnecessary recourse to the death penalty when other bloodless means are sufficient to defend human lives against an aggressor and to protect public order and the safety of persons.

ECCLESIA IN AMERICA
Post-synodal Apostolic Exhortation, January 22, 1999

At the level of human rights, the possibility of human cloning represents a violation of the two fundamental principles on which all human rights are based: the principle of equality among human beings and the principle of nondiscrimination.

HUMAN CLONING IS IMMORAL
Reflections from the Pontifical Academy for Life, July 9, 1997

The Holy See and the Pope have never failed to speak out in order that no one should forget the tragedies which have marked your history and your sufferings. No one can refuse to be concerned with the destiny of so many brothers and sisters in humanity, whose rights are too often not recognized, indeed are often trampled upon. The Holy See has also frequently spoken out on behalf of the security of the State of Israel, being profoundly convinced that security, justice and peace go hand in hand.

TO THE PEOPLE OF PALESTINE, September 22, 1997

Every person is the object of basic rights that are inalienable, inviolable and indivisible. Every person: therefore also the disabled handicapped, who precisely because of their disabilities may encounter greater difficulty in the actual exercise of these rights. Thus they should not be left alone, but be welcomed by society and, according to their abilities, integrated into it as full members.

THE DIGNITY AND RIGHTS OF DISABLED CHILDREN
Address to the Congress The Family and the Integration of Disabled Children and Adolescents, December 4, 1999

Moreover, if it is properly understood, religious freedom will help to ensure the order and common welfare of each nation, of each society, for, when individuals know that their fundamental rights are protected, they are better prepared to work for the common welfare.

THE FREEDOM OF CONSCIENCE AND RELIGIONS, September 1, 1980

You have received, dear indigenous brothers and sisters of America, a rich heritage of human wisdom and at the same time you have been entrusted with your peoples' hopes for the future. The Church, on her part, openly affirms every Christian's right to his own cultural heritage, as something inherent in his dignity as a person and child of God. In its authentic values of truth, goodness and beauty, this heritage must be recognized and respected. Unfortunately, we must admit that the richness of your cultures has not always been appreciated nor have your rights as individuals and peoples been respected. The shadow of sin was cast over America too in the destruction of many of your artistic and cultural creations and in the violence to which you were often subjected.

ADDRESS IN MEXICO TO NATIVE PEOPLES, August 11, 1993

Every human person—no matter how vulnerable or helpless, no matter how young or how old, no matter how healthy, handicapped or sick, no matter how useful or productive for society—is a being of inestimable worth created in the image and likeness of God. This is the dignity of America, the reason she exists, the condition for her survival—yes, the ultimate test of her greatness: to respect every human person, especially the weakest and most defenseless ones, those as yet unborn.

ADDRESS AT DETROIT AIRPORT, September 19, 1987

On this matter [the death penalty] there is a growing tendency, both in the Church and in civil society, to demand that it be applied in a very limited way, or even that it be abolished completely. . . . The nature and extent of the punishment must be carefully evaluated and decided upon, and ought not go to the extreme of executing the offender except in cases of absolute necessity: in other words, when it would not be possible otherwise to defend society. Today, however, as a result of steady improvements in the organization of the penal system, such cases are very rare if not practically nonexistent.

ENCYCLICAL: THE GOSPEL OF LIFE (*Evangelium Vitae*), 1994

The Universal Declaration of Human Rights—with its train of many declarations and conventions on highly important aspects of human rights, in favor of children, of women, of equality between races, and especially the two international covenants on economic, social and cultural rights and on civil and political rights—must remain the basic value in the United Nations organization with which the consciences of its members must be confronted and from which they must draw continual inspiration. If the truths and principles contained in this document were to be forgotten or ignored and were thus to lose the genuine self-evidence that distinguished them at the time they were brought painfully to birth, then the noble purpose of the United Nations organization could be faced with the threat of a new destruction.

ADDRESS TO THE UNITED NATIONS, October 2, 1979

From the theological point of view every baptized person, precisely by reason of being baptized, has the right to receive from the Church instruction and education enabling him or her to enter on a truly Christian life; and from the viewpoint of human rights, every human being has the right to seek religious truth and adhere to it freely, that is to say, "without coercion on the part of individuals or of social groups and any human power," in such a way that in this matter of religion, "no one is to be forced to act against his or her conscience or prevented from acting in conformity to it."

CATECHESIS IN OUR TIME, October 1979

Institutions and laws unjustly ignore the inviolable right of the family and of the human person; and society, far from putting itself at the service of the family, attacks it violently in its values and fundamental requirements. Thus the family, which in God's plan is the basic cell of society and a subject of rights and duties before the state or any other community, finds itself the victim of society, of the delays and slowness with which it acts, and even of its blatant injustice.

For this reason, the Church openly and strongly defends the rights of the family against the intolerable usurpations of society and the state.

APOSTOLIC EXHORTATION *Familiaris Consortio,* 1981

Even in exceptional situations that may at times arise, one can never justify any violation of the fundamental dignity of the human person or of the basic rights that safeguard this dignity. Legitimate concern for the security of a nation, as demanded by the common good, could lead to the temptation of subjugating to the state the human being and his or her dignity and rights. Any apparent conflict between the exigencies of security and of the citizens' basic rights must be resolved according to the fundamental principle—upheld always by the Church—that social organization exists only for the service of man and for the protection of his dignity, and that it cannot claim to serve the common good when human rights are not safeguarded.

ADDRESS AT MANILA, February 17, 1980

Pope John Paul II embraces the spirit of Vatican II when he addresses the role of the laity in the Church today. He encourages lay men and women to take on more responsibilities in the various ministries of the Church. The world encounters the Church through the laity in a distinctive way. Armed with the Living Word, the laity are called to live out their faith in both their Church and secular communities.

The Pope believes that lay people are vital to the mission of the Church. He encourages them to partake actively in the liturgical, educational, and social life of their communities. Through full participation in parish life, lay men and women nourish their brothers and sisters, witnessing the Gospel ideal of faithful service to others. Their efforts as religious educators, eucharistic ministers, pastoral counselors, and diocesan administrators build up the Living Body of Christ. Through the laity, the Church ministers more fully to the complex needs of the faithful.

In secular society, the laity bear witness to the reality of Christ and "permeate [society] with the leaven of the Gospel." In their social, political, intellectual, and economic pursuits, the laity are challenged to imitate Christ. They are called to fulfill a mission: to bring spiritual values to secular life.

John Paul II writes that as "citizens of both the earthly city and the heavenly kingdom," lay Catholics participate in the mission of the Church by receiving the holy sacraments and embodying the message of the Gospel in the world. The laity who respond to this vocation provide an irreplaceable service to the Church and the world.

The Laity

The role of lay people in the mission of the Church extends in two directions: In union with your pastors and assisted by their guidance you build up the communion of the faithful; second, as responsible citizens you permeate with the leaven of the Gospel the society in which you live, in its economic, social, political, cultural and intellectual dimension. When you faithfully carry out these two roles as citizens of both the earthly city and the heavenly kingdom, then are the words of Christ fulfilled: "You are the salt of the earth. . . . You are the light of the world" (Mt 5:13–14).

HOMILY AT ACCRA, GHANA, May 8, 1980

It is their [the laity's] specific vocation and mission to express the Gospel in their lives and thereby to insert the Gospel as a leaven into the reality of the world in which they live and work. The great forces which shape the world—politics, the mass media, science, technology, culture, education, industry and work—are precisely the areas where lay people are especially competent to exercise their mission. If these forces are guided by people who are true disciples of Christ and who are, at the same time, fully competent in the relevant secular knowledge and skill, then indeed will the world be transformed from within by Christ's redeeming power.

HOMILY IN COUNTY LIMERICK, IRELAND, October 1, 1979

In the unity of the Christian life, the various vocations are like so many rays of the one light of Christ, whose radiance "brightens the countenance of the Church." The laity, by virtue of the secular character of their vocation, reflect the mystery of the incarnate Word particularly insofar as He is the Alpha and the Omega of the world, the foundation and measure of the value of all created things. Sacred ministers, for their part, are living images of Christ the head and shepherd, who guides His people during this time of "already and not yet," as they await His coming in glory.

EXHORTATION ON THE CONSECRATED LIFE, March 25, 1996

The development in the United States of what is commonly called lay ministry is certainly a positive and fruitful result of the renewal begun by the Second Vatican Council. Particular attention needs to be paid to the spiritual and doctrinal formation of all lay ministers. In every case they should be men and women of faith, exemplary in personal and family life, who lovingly embrace "the full and complete proclamation of the good news" (*Reconciliatio et Paenitentia*, 9) taught by the Church.

ON PARISHES, LAY MINISTRY AND WOMEN'S ROLES
Ad Limina Address to the U.S. Bishops of Baltimore, Washington,
Atlanta, and Miami, July 2, 1993

Particular care must be given to forming a social conscience at all levels and in all sectors. When injustices worsen and the distance between rich and poor increases distressingly, the social doctrine, in a form which is creative and open to the broad fields of the Church's presence, must be a valuable instrument for formation and action. This holds good particularly for the laity: "It is to the laity, though not exclusively to them, that secular duties and activity properly belong" (GS, 43). It is necessary to avoid supplanting the laity and to study seriously just when certain forms of assistance to them retain their reason for existence. Is it not the laity who are called, by reason of their vocation in the Church, to make their contribution in the political and economic dimensions, and to be effectively present in the safeguarding and advancement of human rights?

ADDRESS TO LATIN AMERICAN BISHOPS AT PUEBLA,
February 8, 1979

The mission of the Church in the world is accomplished not only by ministers who have received the sacrament of orders, but also by all the lay faithful. Because they have been baptized, the lay faithful share in the priestly, prophetic and royal functions of Christ.

ADDRESS AT RÉUNION, May 30, 1989

Your Christian vocation does not take you away from any of your other brothers and sisters. It does not inhibit your involvement in civic affairs nor exempt you from your responsibilities as a citizen. It does not divide you from society nor relieve you of the daily trials of life. Rather your continued engagement in secular activities and professions is truly a part of your vocation. For you are called to make the Church present and fruitful in the ordinary circumstances of life—in married and family life, in the daily conditions of earning a living, in political and civic responsibilities and in cultural, scientific and educational pursuits. No human activity is foreign to the Gospel. God wishes all of creation to be ordered to His kingdom, and it is especially to the laity that the Lord has entrusted this task.

HOMILY AT ACCRA, GHANA, May 8, 1980

To perform a Church calling as lay men and women often means giving clear witness to the Church against the customary social habits of ordinary living. It means having to bring the demands of the Church calling, the demands of the family and the demands of one's personal life into harmony. You can achieve this through living more consciously from the springs of your life, by the Holy Spirit, the springs which you received in your baptism and confirmation.

ADDRESS TO LAY CHURCH WORKERS IN WEST GERMANY,
November 18, 1980

You who are lay persons in the Church and who possess faith, the greatest of all resources—you have a unique opportunity and crucial responsibility. Through your lives in the midst of your daily activities in the world, you show the power that faith has to transform the world and to renew the family of man.

HOMILY AT ACCRA, GHANA, May 8, 1980

It is a blessing for the Church that in so many parishes the lay faithful assist priests in a variety of ways: in religious education, pastoral counseling, social service activities, administration, etc. This increased participation is undoubtedly a work of the Spirit renewing the Church's vigor.

ON PARISHES, LAY MINISTRY AND WOMEN'S ROLES
Ad Limina Address to the U.S. Bishops of Baltimore,
Washington, Atlanta, and Miami, July 2, 1993

As members of the laity, you are called to take an active part in the sacramental and liturgical life of the Church, especially in the eucharistic sacrifice. At the same time you are called to spread the Gospel actively through the practice of charity and through involvement in catechetical and missionary efforts, according to the gifts which each one of you has received (cf. 1 Cor 12:4ff).

HOMILY AT ACCRA, GHANA, May 8, 1980

The Christian faith does not provide you with ready-made solutions to the complex problems affecting contemporary society. But it does give you deep insights into the nature of man and his needs, calling you to speak the truth in love, to take up your responsibilities as good citizens and to work with your neighbors to build a society where true human values are nourished and deepened by a shared Christian vision of life.

HOMILY AT NAIROBI, KENYA, May 7, 1980

Although John Paul affirms that human erotic impulses are a gift of God, they are nevertheless not the basis for love. Love must be a true gift of the self to another, and cannot be based on the selfishness implied in the mere satisfaction of sexual desire. John Paul does not reject erotic delight, but he does condemn lust—false eroticism—as the attraction toward a partial good, instead of toward the complete value of another person created in the image of God. He also encourages self-restraint in resisting impulses that arise from mere carnality because acts based on such impulses are devoid of conscious choice.

We are images of God not only in our minds and spirits but in our physical bodies as well. John Paul affirms that the human body and its sexual drives are potentially good, and an individual among other individuals finds his way to God either through the responsible love of another human in marriage or by being called as a practicer of celibacy or upholder of virginity.

John Paul emphasizes that real love is difficult and demanding, and that love—between men and women, parents and children, friends, even between nations and peoples—requires self-sacrifice and self-discipline. In the end, however, love is richly rewarded with joy.

Love

Man cannot live without love. He remains a being that is incomprehensible for himself, his life is senseless, if love is not revealed to him, if he does not encounter love, if he does not experience it and make it his own, if he does not participate intimately in it. This, as has already been said, is why Christ the Redeemer "fully reveals man to himself." If we may use the expression, this is the human dimension of the mystery of the Redemption.

ENCYCLICAL: THE REDEEMER OF MAN (*Redemptor Hominis*), 1979

Love your neighbor as yourself. This saying surely strikes a chord in your hearts, dear Government Leaders, Members of Parliament, Politicians and Public Administrators. To each of you, today, on the occasion of your Jubilee, it poses a fundamental question: how, in your delicate and demanding service to the state and to its citizens, can you carry out this commandment? The answer is clear: by living your involvement in politics as a service to others. An approach as magnificent as it is demanding! It cannot in fact be reduced to some generic restatement of principles or a declaration of good intentions. Political service is lived in a precise and daily commitment, which calls for great competence in the fulfillment of one's duties and unswerving morality in the selfless and accountable exercise of power.

ADDRESS AT THE JUBILEE OF GOVERNMENT LEADERS, MEMBERS OF PARLIAMENT, AND POLITICIANS, November 4, 2000

This sister [Mother Teresa], universally known as the Mother of the Poor, leaves an eloquent example for everyone, believer and nonbeliever. She leaves us the witness of God's love, which she accepted and which transformed her life into a total gift to her brothers and sisters. She leaves us the witness of contempation which becomes love, of love which becomes contemplation. The works she accomplished speak for themselves and show the people of our time that lofty meaning of life which unfortunately seems often to be lost.

REFLECTIONS BEFORE RECITING THE ANGELUS, September 7, 1997

The sickness of a family member, friend or neighbor is a call to Christians to demonstrate true compassion, that gentle and persevering sharing in another's pain. Likewise, the handicapped and those who are ill must never feel that they are a burden; they are persons being visited by the Lord.

AMERICA: BE HOSPITABLE TO LIFE
Ad Limina Address to U.S. Bishops, October 2, 1998

The terminally ill in particular deserve the solidarity, communion and affection of those around them; they often need to be able to forgive and to be forgiven, to make peace with God and with others.

AMERICA: BE HOSPITABLE TO LIFE
Ad Limina Address to U.S. Bishops, October 2, 1998

Although everything seems to confirm that love is a thing "of the world," that it is born in souls and bodies as the fruit of emotional sensitivity and sensuous attraction, reaching to the hidden depths of the sexual constitution of the organism, yet through all this and as if over and above all this, love is a gift.

FRUITFUL AND RESPONSIBLE LOVE, 1979

Above all, hold high the esteem for the wonderful dignity and grace of the sacrament of marriage. Prepare earnestly for it. Believe in the spiritual power which this sacrament of Jesus Christ gives to strengthen the marriage union and to overcome all the crises and problems of life together.

Married people must believe in the power of the sacrament to make them holy. They must believe in their vocation to witness through their marriage to the power of Christ's love. True love and the grace of God can never let marriage become a self-centered relationship of two individuals, living side by side for their own interests.

LETTER TO FAMILIES FOR THE INTERNATIONAL YEAR
OF THE FAMILY, February 22, 1994

Within this same cultural climate, the body is no longer perceived as a properly personal reality, a sign and place of relations with others, with God and with the world. It is reduced to pure materiality: It is simply a complex of organs, functions and energies to be used according to the sole criteria of pleasure and efficiency. Consequently, sexuality too is depersonalized and exploited: From being the sign, place and language of love, that is, of the gift of self and acceptance of another in all the other's richness as a person, it increasingly becomes the occasion and instrument for self-assertion and the selfish satisfaction of personal desires and instincts. Thus the original import of human sexuality is distorted and falsified, and the two meanings, unitive and procreative, inherent in the very nature of the conjugal act are artificially separated: In this way the marriage union is betrayed and its fruitfulness is subjected to the caprice of the couple.

ENCYCLICAL: THE GOSPEL OF LIFE (*Evangelium Vitae*), 1994

The central value, upon which other values in love depend, is the value of the human person. It is to the human person that basic responsibility refers. The texts of the Second Vatican Council affirm many times that love in general, and conjugal love in particular, consists in the gift of one person to another, a gift that embraces the human being as a whole, soul and body. Such a gift presupposes that the person as such has a unique value for the other person, which expresses itself in a particular responsibility for that value, precisely because of its degree and because of its intensity, so to speak. And through a responsibility thus conceived there is formed the essential structure of marriage, a bond at once spiritual and moral.

FRUITFUL AND RESPONSIBLE LOVE, 1979

So often the pressures of modern living separate husbands and wives from one another, threatening their lifelong interdependence of love and fidelity. Can we also not be concerned about the impact of cultural pressures upon relations between the generations, upon parental authority and the transmission of sacred values? Our Christian conscience should be deeply concerned about the way in which sins against love and against life are often presented as examples of "progress" and emancipation. Most often, are they not but the age-old forms of selfishness dressed up in a new language and presented in a new cultural framework?

BUILDING UP THE BODY OF CHRIST
Pastoral Visit to the United States, 1987

In fact it is one thing to be conscious that the value of sex is a part of all the rich storehouse of values with which the female appears to the male; it is another to "reduce" all the personal riches of femininity to that single value, that is, as a suitable object of gratification of sexuality itself. The same reasoning can be valid concerning what masculinity is for the woman.

BLESSED ARE THE PURE OF HEART
General Audience, September 17, 1980

Conjugal love is fulfilled by parenthood. Responsibility for this love from the beginning to the end is at the same time responsibility also for parenthood. The one participates in the other, and they both constitute each other. Parenthood is a gift that comes to people, to man and to woman, together with love, that creates a perspective of love in the dimension of a reciprocal lifelong self-giving, and that is the condition of gradual realization of that perspective through life and action.

FRUITFUL AND RESPONSIBLE LOVE, 1979

Real love is demanding. I would fail in my mission if I did not clearly tell you so. For it was Jesus—our Jesus Himself—who said, "You are my friends if you do what I command you" (Jn 15:14). Love demands effort and a personal commitment to the will of God. It means discipline and sacrifice, but it also means joy and human fulfillment.

ADDRESS AT BOSTON, October 1, 1979

The message of love that Christ brought is always important, always relevant. It is not difficult to see how today's world, despite its beauty and grandeur, despite the conquests of science and technology, despite the refined and abundant material good that it offers, is yearning for more truth, for more love, for more joy. And all of this is found in Christ and His way of life.

ADDRESS AT BOSTON, October 1, 1979

For John Paul, the essential mission of the family is to create an atmosphere in which love can flourish. In this, the family imitates the bond of love that ties Christ to the members of the Church. In fact, the family is a church in miniature, a domestic church with its own mission.

John Paul sees two opposing forces at work today that affect the family. On the one hand, there is greater attempt to ensure personal freedom and examine the quality of relationships, which includes assuring the dignity and equality of women and children. On the other, he notices a disturbing degradation of some fundamental values: mistaken ideas of the meaning of individual freedom of the spouses, confusion about the authority of parents over children, and an increase in divorce and abortion.

The Holy Father urges Catholics to use the family as the first school of social life, an example of how to live in the broader community; and he specifically instructs families to dedicate themselves to social service, especially on behalf of the poor. He reminds parents that these activities should involve the children as well, in the measure that age and ability allow them to participate.

Parents are the first and most important educators of their children, and this is a role they can never abdicate. Children need acceptance, love, esteem, spiritual and emotional support, and also the material comfort that makes healthy childhood possible. Nor can the elderly be forgotten, and John Paul observes that certain nonindustrial cultures do much better than some in the industrial world in assuring the elderly a proper and dignified place in the life of the family.

MARRIAGE AND THE FAMILY

The bond that unites a family is not only a matter of natural kinship or of shared life and experience. It is essentially a holy and religious bond. Marriage and the family are sacred realities.

BUILDING UP THE BODY OF CHRIST
Pastoral Visit to the United States, 1987

The family is *the first setting of evangelization,* the place where the Good News of Christ is first received, and then, in simple yet profound ways handed on from generation to generation. At the same time, families in our time finally depend upon the Church to defend their rights and to teach the obligations and responsibilities which lead to the fullness of joy and life. Thus, I urge all of you, especially the clergy, to teach the obligations and responsibilities which lead to the fullness of joy and life. Thus, I urge all of you, especially the clergy and the Religious, to work for the promotion of family values within the local community.

ADDRESS AT NEW ORLEANS, September 12, 1987

Giving life and helping their children to reach maturity through education are among the primary privileges and responsibilities of married couples. We know that married couples usually look forward to parenthood but are sometimes impeded from achieving their hopes and desires by social conditions, by personal circumstances or even by inability to beget life. But the Church encourages couples to be generous and hopeful, to realize that parenthood is a privilege and that each child bears witness to the couple's own love for each other, to their generosity and to their openness to God. They must be encouraged to see the child as an enrichment of their marriage and a gift of God to themselves and to their other children.

Ad Limina ADDRESS TO U.S. BISHOPS, September 24, 1983

Christian families exist to form a communion of persons in love. As such, the Church and the family are each in its own way living representations in human history of the eternal loving communion of the three persons of the Most Holy Trinity. In fact, the family is called the Church in miniature, "the domestic church," a particular expression of the Church through the human experience of love and common life.

ADDRESS AT COLUMBIA, SOUTH CAROLINA, September 11, 1987

I address you, Christian families. Parents, give thanks to the Lord if He has called one of your children to the consecrated life. It is to be considered a great honor—as it always has been—that the Lord should look upon a family and choose to invite one of its members to set out on the path of the evangelical counsels! Cherish the desire to give the Lord one of your children so that God's love can spread in the world. What fruit of conjugal love could be more beautiful than this?

EXHORTATION ON THE CONSECRATED LIFE, March 25, 1996

Pushed onward by the euphoria of hedonism, the affluent society has offered sex for sale, sex as entertainment and a leisure-time activity outside the family, without a vision inspired by the good of the person but by consumerism. The mass media, pornography and erotic telephone services have given children the emotional impetus to enter the market, where they are regarded more as the object rather than the subject of the alienating mechanisms.

GUIDELINES FOR SEXUAL EDUCATION FOR THE FAMILY,
February 14, 1996

While in the natural order sex was understood as being connected with its responsible use in the family, in the sixties a "revolution" began. In the beginning it seemed to be an expression of emancipation, of liberation from sexual taboos, in order to gain recognition for the right to pleasure, free from any responsibility. It is true that this tendency is as old as humanity itself; however, it seems that the new feature lies in the effort to justify this transition from the responsible use of sex to the search for selfish pleasure. This not only introduces the separation between sexual expression, the act and its meaning, but it entails a breakdown in the area of relationships.

GUIDELINES FOR SEXUAL EDUCATION FOR THE FAMILY,
February 14, 1996

We grieve over the brokenness of so many families in all classes, and we offer to you our prayers. To you single parents who, with trust in God, bravely assume the responsibility of raising children in the Christian life without the companionship and support of a spouse, we extend the encouragement of the family of faith.

ENCOUNTER WITH JESUS: CONVERSIONS, COMMUNION AND
SOLIDARITY
Message of the Special Assembly for America of the Synod of Bishops,
December 9, 1997

It is necessary to reaffirm that ratified and consummated sacramental marriage can never be dissolved, not even by the power of the Roman pontiff. The opposite assertion would imply the thesis that there is no absolutely indissoluble marriage, which would be contrary to what the Church has taught and still teaches about the indissolubility of the marital bond.

THE INDISSOLUBILITY OF MARRIAGE AND THE MENTALITY
OF DIVORCE
Address to Prelate Auditors, Officials, and Advocates of the Tribunal
of the Roman Rota, January 21, 2000

The Roman pontiff in fact has the "*sacra potestas*" to teach the truth of the Gospel, administer the sacraments and pastorally govern the Church in the name and with the authority of Christ, but this power does not include per se any power over the divine law, natural or positive. Neither Scripture nor Tradition recognizes any faculty of the Roman pontiff for dissolving a ratified and consummated marriage; on the contrary, the Church's constant practice shows the certain knowledge of Tradition that such a power does not exist.

THE INDISSOLUBILITY OF MARRIAGE AND THE MENTALITY
OF DIVORCE
Address to Prelate Auditors, Officials, and Advocates of the Tribunal
of the Roman Rota, January 21, 2000

The arrival of a suffering child is certainly a disconcerting event for families, who are left deeply shocked by it. From this point of view, too, it is important to encourage parents to devote special attention . . . to the children, by developing a profound esteem for their personal dignity, and a great respect and generous concern for their rights. This is true for every child, but it becomes all the more urgent the smaller the child is and the more it is in need of everything, when it is sick, suffering or handicapped.

THE DIGNITY AND RIGHTS OF DISABLED CHILDREN
Address to the Congress The Family and the Integration of Disabled Children and Adolescents, December 4, 1999

Parents must be encouraged to face this far-from-easy situation without turning in on themselves. It is important that the problem be shared not only with close relatives, but also with qualified persons and friends. These are the "Good Samaritans" of our time who, by their generous and friendly presence, repeat the gesture of Christ, who always made his comforting closeness felt by the sick and by those in difficulty.

THE DIGNITY AND RIGHTS OF DISABLED CHILDREN
Address to the Congress The Family and the Integration of Disabled Children and Adolescents, December 4, 1999

Despite the generous efforts of so many, however, the idea that elective abortion is a "right" continues to be asserted. Moreover, there are signs of an almost unimaginable insensitivity to the reality of what actually happens during an abortion, as evidenced in recent events surrounding so-called partial-birth abortion. This is a cause for deep concern. A society with a diminished sense of the value of human life at its earliest stages has already opened the door to a culture of death.

AMERICA: BE HOSPITABLE TO LIFE
Ad Limina Address to U.S. Bishops, October 2, 1998

Acceptance, love, esteem, many-sided and united material, emotional, educational and spiritual concern for every child that comes into this world should always constitute a distinctive, essential characteristic of all Christians, in particular of the Christian family: Thus children, while they are able to grow "in wisdom and in stature, and in favor with God and man" offer their own precious contribution to building up the family community and even to the sanctification of their parents.

APOSTOLIC EXHORTATION *Familiaris Consortio*, 1981

The family is set at the very center of common good in its various dimensions, precisely because man is conceived and born in it. Everything possible must be done in order that this human being may be desired, awaited, experienced as a particular, unique and unrepeatable value, right from the beginning, from the moment of his conception. He must feel that he is important, useful, dear and of great value, even if infirm or handicapped; even dearer in fact for this reason.

THE FAMILY: CENTER OF LOVE AND LIFE
General Audience, January 3, 1979

The domestic virtues, based upon a profound respect for human life and dignity, and practiced in understanding, patience, mutual encouragement and forgiveness, enable the community of the family to live out the first and fundamental experience of peace.

THE FAMILY CREATES THE PEACE OF THE HUMAN FAMILY
Message for World Day of Peace, January 1, 1994

The Pharaoh of old, haunted by the presence and increase of the children of Israel, submitted them to every kind of oppression and ordered that every male child born of the Hebrew women was to be killed (cf. Ex 1:7–22). Today, not a few of the powerful of the earth act in the same way. They too are haunted by the current demographic growth and fear that the most prolific and poorest peoples represent a threat for the well-being and peace of their own countries. Consequently, rather than wishing to face and solve these serious problems with respect for the dignity of individuals and families and for every person's inviolable right to life, they prefer to promote and impose by whatever means a massive program of birth control. Even the economic help which they would be ready to give is unjustly made conditional on the acceptance of antibirth policy.

ENCYCLICAL: THE GOSPEL OF LIFE (*Evangelium Vitae*), 1994

Christian marriage, like the other sacraments, "whose purpose is to sanctify people, to build up the body of Christ, and finally, to give worship to God" is in itself a liturgical action glorifying God in Jesus Christ and in the Church. By celebrating it, Christian spouses profess their gratitude to God for the sublime gift bestowed on them of being able to live in their married and family lives the very love of God for people and that of the Lord Jesus for the Church, His bride.

APOSTOLIC EXHORTATION *Familiaris Consortio*, 1981

I have spoken of two closely related yet not identical concepts: the concept of communion and that of community. Communion has to do with the personal relationship between the I and the thou. Community, on the other hand, transcends this framework and moves toward a society, a we. The family, as á community of persons, is thus the first human society. It arises whenever there comes into being the conjugal covenant of marriage, which opens the spouses to a lasting communion of love and of life, and it is brought to completion in a full and specific way with the procreation of children: the communion of the spouses gives rise to the community of the family. The community of the family is completely pervaded by the very essence of communion. On the human level, can there be any other communion comparable to that between a mother and a child whom she has carried in her womb and then brought to birth?

LETTER TO FAMILIES FOR THE INTERNATIONAL YEAR
OF THE FAMILY, February 22, 1994

In order that Christian marriage may favor the total good and development of the married couple, it must be inspired by the Gospel, and thus be open to new life—new life to be given and accepted generously. The couple is also called to create a family atmosphere in which children can be happy and lead full and worthy human and Christian lives.

HOMILY AT THE WASHINGTON MALL, October 7, 1979

Experience teaches that human love, which naturally tends toward fatherhood and motherhood, is sometimes affected by a profound crisis and is thus seriously threatened. In such cases help can be sought at marriage and family counseling centers where it is possible, among other things, to obtain the assistance of specifically trained psychologists and psychotherapists. At the same time, however, we cannot forget the perennial validity of the words of the apostle: "I bow my knees before the Father, from whom every family in heaven and on earth is named." Marriage, the sacrament of matrimony, is a covenant of persons in love. And love can be deepened and preserved only by love, that love which is "poured into our hearts through the Holy Spirit which has been given to us" (Rom 5:5).

LETTER TO FAMILIES FOR THE INTERNATIONAL YEAR
OF THE FAMILY, February 22, 1994

In the conviction that the good of the family is an indispensable and essential value of the civil community, the public authorities must do everything possible to ensure that families have all those aids—economic, social, educational, political and cultural assistance—that they need in order to face all their responsibilities in a human way.

APOSTOLIC EXHORTATION *Familiaris Consortio*, 1981

Authentic conjugal love presupposes and requires that a man have a profound respect for the equal dignity of his wife: "You are not her master," writes St. Ambrose, "but her husband; she was not given to you to be your slave, but your wife. . . . Reciprocate her attentiveness to you and be grateful to her for her love." With his wife a man should live "a very special form of personal friendship." As for the Christian, he is called upon to develop a new attitude of love, manifesting toward his wife a charity that is both gentle and strong like that which Christ has for the Church.

APOSTOLIC EXHORTATION *Familiaris Consortio*, 1981

Sexuality, by means of which man and woman give themselves to one another through the acts which are proper and exclusive to spouses, is by no means something purely biological, but concerns the innermost being of the human person as such. It is realized in a truly human way only if it is an integral part of the love by which a man and a woman commit themselves totally to one another until death.

APOSTOLIC EXHORTATION *Familiaris Consortio*, 1981

The Church condemns as a grave offense against human dignity and justice all those activities of governments or other public authorities which attempt to limit in any way the freedom of couples in deciding about children. Consequently, any violence applied by such authorities in favor of contraception or, still worse, of sterilization and procured abortion must be altogether condemned and forcefully rejected. Likewise to be denounced as gravely unjust are cases where in international relations economic help given for the advancement of peoples is made conditional on programs of contraception, sterilization and procured abortion.

APOSTOLIC EXHORTATION *Familiaris Consortio*, 1981

The family, as the fundamental and essential educating community, is the privileged means for transmitting the religious and cultural values which help the person to acquire his or her own identity. Founded on love and open to the gift of life, the family contains in itself the very future of society; its most special task is to contribute effectively to a future peace.

THE FAMILY CREATES THE PEACE OF THE HUMAN FAMILY
Message for World Day of Peace, January 1, 1994

The deepest human problems are connected with the family. It constitutes the primary, fundamental and irreplaceable community for man.

THE FAMILY: CENTER OF LOVE AND LIFE
General Audience, December 31, 1978

The Holy Father sees modern man's moral conflicts as growing out of a misunderstanding of individualism, in which each person measures nothing but his own advantage, and counts himself free to enthusiastically pursue any behavior in his self-interest "as long as I don't hurt anyone else." The Pope finds this a totally inadequate condition for moral conduct.

Self-giving and self-surrender form the model for successful family life and describe the proper relationship between husbands and wives, children and parents, older and younger generations. This is also the model for justice and morality in the wider world. Yet justice is not a legal contract. While we must understand that others have the same rights as we do, such understanding is not sufficient. John Paul emphasizes that true justice lies in recognizing that others have not only rights but also needs, and that all of God's children are deserving of having those needs fulfilled.

In relations between people, the ultimate lack of morality is to treat another as an object: to ask, "What can he or she do for me?" Selfishness and a misguided individualism are fatal to human dignity. The Lord Himself, who came "to serve rather than be served," offers the pattern of living that leads to Eternal Life.

MORALITY

It becomes necessary, therefore, on the part of all to recover an awareness of the primacy of moral values, which are the values of the human person as such. The great task that has to be faced today for the renewal of society is that of recapturing the ultimate meaning of life and its fundamental values.

APOSTOLIC EXHORTATION *Familiaris Consortio*, 1981

Every age poses new challenges and new temptations for the People of God on their pilgrimage, and ours is no exception. We face a growing secularism that tries to exclude God and religious truth from human affairs. We face an insidious relativism that undermines the absolute truth of Christ and the truths of faith, and tempts believers to think of them as merely one set of beliefs or opinions among others. We face a materialistic consumerism that offers a whole series of pleasures that will never satisfy the human heart. All these attitudes can influence our sense of good and evil at the very moment when social and scientific progress requires strong ethical guidance. Once alienated from Christian faith and practice by these and other deceptions, people often commit themselves to passing fads, or to bizarre beliefs that are either shallow or fanatical.

ADDRESS AT MONTEREY, CALIFORNIA, September 17, 1987

In the twenty-five years which have passed since the judicial decision legalizing abortion in your country there has been a widespread mobilization of consciences in support of life. The pro-life movement is one of the most positive aspects of American public life, and the support given it by the bishops is a tribute to your pastoral leadership.

AMERICA: BE HOSPITABLE TO LIFE
Ad Limina Address to U.S. Bishops, October 2, 1998

Democracy cannot be sustained without a shared commitment to certain moral truths about the human person and human community. The basic question before a democratic society is: "How ought we to live together?" In seeking an answer to this question, can society exclude moral truth and moral reasoning? Can the biblical wisdom which played such a formative part in the very founding of your country be excluded from that debate? Would not doing so mean that America's founding documents no longer have any defining content, but are only the formal dressing of changing opinion? Would not doing so mean that tens of millions of Americans could no longer offer the contribution of their deepest convictions to the formation of public policy? Surely it is important for America that the moral truths which make freedom possible should be passed on to each new generation.

HOMILY AT MASS IN CAMDEN YARDS, BALTIMORE, August 8, 1995

As the experience of the past twenty-five years has shown, legalized abortion has been a destructive force in the lives of many individuals, especially women who are often left alone to bear the deep sorrow and regret which follow the decision to destroy the life of an unborn child. But the proliferation of procured abortions has also had deleterious effects on society at large, not least in a weakening of respect for the life of the elderly and the infirm, and a coarsening of the moral sense. When the killing of the innocent is sanctioned by law, the distinction between good and evil is obscured and society is led to justify even such clearly immoral procedures as partial-birth abortion.

TWENTY-FIFTH ANNIVERSARY OF *ROE V. WADE*
Message to Cardinal Bernard Law,
Archbishop of Boston, December 29, 1997

Catholic moral teaching sheds a guiding light on questions connected with the delicate process of life's dawning, so full of hope and rich in promise for later life, and a field now ripe for the marvelous discoveries of medical science. I trust that your work will always be inspired by a clear recognition of the dignity proper to every human being, each of whom is an incomparable gift of the creative love of God.

THE ETHICS OF FETAL THERAPY
Address to the International Congress The Fetus as a Patient,
April 3, 2000

To welcome the weakest, helping them on their journey, is a sign of civilization.

THE DIGNITY AND RIGHTS OF DISABLED CHILDREN
Address to the Congress The Family and the Integration of Disabled
Children and Adolescents, December 4, 1999

Respect for the rights of conscience is deeply ingrained in your national culture, which was formed in part by emigrants who came to the New World to vindicate their religious and moral convictions in the face of persecution. American society's historic admiration for men and women of conscience is the ground on which you can teach the truth about conscience today.

MORAL TRUTH, CONSCIENCE AND AMERICAN DEMOCRACY
Ad Limina Address to U.S. Bishops, June 27, 1998

A society or culture which wishes to survive cannot declare the spiritual dimension of the human person to be irrelevant to public life.

MORAL TRUTH, CONSCIENCE AND AMERICAN DEMOCRACY
Ad Limina Address to U.S. Bishops, June 27, 1998

Your country prides itself on being a realized democracy, but democracy is itself a moral adventure, a continuing test of a people's capacity to govern themselves in ways that serve the common good and the good of individual citizens. The survival of a particular democracy depends not only on its institutions, but to an even greater extent on the spirit which inspires and permeates its procedures for legislating, administering and judging.

MORAL TRUTH, CONSCIENCE AND AMERICAN DEMOCRACY
Ad Limina Address to U.S. Bishops, June 27, 1998

If there is no objective standard to help adjudicate between different conceptions of the personal and common good, then democratic politics is reduced to a raw contest for power. If constitutional and statutory law are not held accountable to the objective moral law, the first casualties are justice and equity, for they become matters of personal opinion.

MORAL TRUTH, CONSCIENCE AND AMERICAN DEMOCRACY
Ad Limina Address to U.S. Bishops, June 27, 1998

A climate of moral relativism is incompatible with democracy. That kind of culture cannot answer questions fundamental to a democratic political community: Why should I regard my fellow citizen as my equal? Why should I defend someone else's rights? Why should I work for the common good? If moral truths cannot be publicly acknowledged as such, democracy is impossible.

MORAL TRUTH, CONSCIENCE AND AMERICAN DEMOCRACY
Ad Limina Address to U.S. Bishops, June 27, 1998

The Church likewise offers a truly vital service to the nation when she awakens public awareness to the morally objectionable nature of campaigns for the legalization of physician-assisted suicide and euthanasia. Euthanasia and suicide are grave violations of God's law; their legalization introduces a direct threat to the persons least capable of defending themselves and it proves most harmful to the democratic institutions of society.

AMERICA: BE HOSPITABLE TO LIFE
Ad Limina Address to U.S. Bishops, October 2, 1998

As ecumenical witness in defense of life develops, a great teaching effort is needed to clarify the substantive moral difference between discontinuing medical procedures that may be burdensome, dangerous or disproportionate to the expected outcome—what the Catechism of the Catholic Church calls "the refusal of 'overzealous' treatment"—and taking away the ordinary means of preserving life, such as feeding, hydration and normal medical care.

AMERICA: BE HOSPITABLE TO LIFE
Ad Limina Address to U.S. Bishops, October 2, 1998

The drug trade, the recycling of illicit funds, corruption at every level, the terror of violence, the arms race, racial discrimination, inequality between social groups and the irrational destruction of nature . . . these sins are the sign of a deep crisis caused by the loss of a sense of God and the absence of those moral principles which should guide the life of every person. In the absence of moral points of reference, an unbridled greed for wealth and power takes over, obscuring any Gospel-based vision of social reality.

ECCLESIA IN AMERICA
Post-synodal Apostolic Exhortation, January 22, 1999

Forgiveness demonstrates the presence in the world of the love which is more powerful than sin. Forgiveness is also the fundamental condition for reconciliation, not only in the relationship of God with man, but also in relationships between people. A world from which forgiveness was eliminated would be nothing but a world of cold and unfeeling justice in the name of which each person would claim his or her own rights vis-à-vis others; the various kinds of selfishness latent in man would transform life and human society into a system of oppression of the weak by the strong, or into an arena of permanent strife between one group and another.

ENCYCLICAL: MERCY OF GOD (Dives in Misericordia), 1980

Why is life a good? This question is found everywhere in the Bible, and from the very first pages it receives a powerful and amazing answer. The life which God gives man is quite different from the life of all other living creatures inasmuch as man, although formed from the dust of the earth (cf. Gn 2:7, 3:19, Jb 34:15; Ps 103:14, 104:29), is a manifestation of God in the world, a sign of his presence, a trace of his glory (cf. Gn 1:26–27; Ps 8:6).

ENCYCLICAL: THE GOSPEL OF LIFE (Evangelium Vitae), 1994

Lust, and in particular the lust of the body, is a specific threat to the structure of self-control and self-mastery, through which the human person is formed.

BLESSED ARE THE PURE OF HEART
General Audience, May 28, 1980

To claim the right to abortion, infanticide and euthanasia, and to recognize that right in law, means to attribute to human freedom a perverse and evil significance: that of an absolute power over others and against others. This is the death of true freedom: "Truly, truly, I say to you, everyone who commits sin is a slave to sin" (Jn 8:34).

ENCYCLICAL: THE GOSPEL OF LIFE (Evangelium Vitae), 1994

Among your many activities at the service of life there is one which, especially at this juncture of history, deserves our firmest support: it is the continuing struggle against what the Second Vatican Council calls "the abominable crime" of abortion (Gaudeam et Spes, 51). Disregard for the sacred character of life in the womb weakens the very fabric of the acceptance of other practices that are against the fundamental rights of the individual.

SPEECH TO BISHOPS AT LOS ANGELES, September 1987

Many of the problems [of modern life] are the result of a false notion of individual freedom at work in our culture, as if we could be free only when rejecting every objective norm of conduct, refusing to assume responsibility or even refusing to put curbs on instincts and passions! Instead, true freedom implies that we are capable of choosing a good without constraint. This is the truly human way of proceeding in the choices—big and small—which life puts before us.

ADDRESS AT COLUMBIA, SOUTH CAROLINA, September 11, 1987

Nothing "from outside" makes man filthy, no "material" dirt makes man impure in the moral, that is, interior sense. No ablution, not even of a ritual nature, is capable in itself of producing moral purity. This has its exclusive source within man; it comes from the heart.

BLESSED ARE THE PURE OF HEART
General Audience, December 10, 1980

In the materialistic perspective . . . interpersonal relations are seriously impoverished. The first to be harmed are women, children, the sick or suffering and the elderly. The criterion of personal dignity—which demands respect, generosity and service—is replaced by the criterion of efficiency, functionality and usefulness: Others are considered not for what they "are," but for what they "have, do and produce." This is the supremacy of the strong over the weak.

ENCYCLICAL: THE GOSPEL OF LIFE (*Evangelium Vitae*), 1994

Faced with problems and disappointments, many people will try to escape from their responsibility: escape in selfishness, escape in sexual pleasure, escape in drugs, escape in violence, escape in indifference and cynical attitudes. But today, I propose to you the option of love, which is the opposite of escape.

ADDRESS AT BOSTON, October 1, 1979

The Christian faith and the Christian Church don't object to the depiction of evil in its various forms. Evil is a reality whose extent has been experienced and suffered in this century in the extreme by your country and mine. Without the reality of evil, the reality of good, redemption, mercy and salvation cannot be measured. This is not a license for evil, but rather an indication of its position.

ADDRESS AT MUNICH, November 19, 1980

The Church, having before her eyes the picture of the generation to which we belong, shares the uneasiness of so many of the people of our time. Moreover, one cannot fail to be worried by the decline of many fundamental values, which constitute an unquestionable good not only for Christian morality but simply for human morality, for moral culture: these values include respect for human life from the moment of conception, respect for marriage in its indissoluble unity and respect for the stability of the family.

ENCYCLICAL: MERCY OF GOD (*Dives in Misericordia*), 1980

Mercy in itself, as a perfection of the infinite God, is also infinite. Also infinite therefore and inexhaustible is the Father's readiness to receive the prodigal children who return to His home. Infinite are the readiness and power of forgiveness which flow continually from the marvelous value of the sacrifice of the Son. No human sin can prevail over this power or even limit it.

ENCYCLICAL: MERCY OF GOD (*Dives in Misericordia*), 1980

On a more general level, there exists in contemporary culture a certain Promethean attitude which leads people to think that they can control life and death by taking the decisions about them into their own hands. What really happens in this case is that the individual is overcome and crushed by a death deprived of any prospect of meaning or hope. We see a tragic expression of all this in the spread of euthanasia—disguised and surreptitious or practiced openly and even legally.

ENCYCLICAL: THE GOSPEL OF LIFE (*Evangelium Vitae*), 1994

One of the key pastoral problems facing us is the widespread misunderstanding of the role of conscience, whereby individual conscience and experience are exalted above or against Church teaching. The young women and men of America, and indeed of the whole Western world, who are often victims of educational theories which propose that they "create" their own values and that "feeling good about themselves" is a primary guiding moral principle, are asking to be led out of this moral confusion.

Ad Limina ADDRESS TO U.S. BISHOPS FROM NEW ENGLAND,
September 21, 1993

In a technological culture in which people are used to dominating matter, discovering its laws and mechanisms in order to transform it according to their wishes, the danger arises of also wanting to manipulate conscience and its demands. In a culture which holds that no universally valid truths are possible, nothing is absolute. Therefore, in the end—they say—objective goodness and evil no longer really matter. Good comes to mean what is pleasing or useful at a particular moment. Evil means what contradicts our subjective wishes. Each person can build a private system of values.

PRAYER VIGIL AT WORLD YOUTH DAY, August 26, 1993

A temperate man is one who does not abuse food, drinks, pleasures; who does not drink alcoholic beverages to excess; who does not deprive himself of consciousness by using drugs or narcotics. We can imagine within us a "lower self" and a "higher self." In our "lower self" our "body" is expressed with its needs, its desires, its passions of sensible nature. The virtue of temperance guarantees every man the control of the "lower self" by the "higher self." Is it a question, in this case, of a humiliation, a disability, for our body? On the contrary! This control gives it new value, exalts it.

VATICAN ADDRESS, November 22, 1978

The greatest obstacle to man's journey toward God is sin, perseverance in sin and, finally, denial of God—the deliberate blotting out of God from the world of human thought, the detachment from Him of the whole of man's earthly activity, the rejection of God by man.

THE MESSAGE OF FATIMA, May 13, 1982

The man of today seems ever to be under threat from what he produces, that is to say from the result of the work of his hands and, even more so, of the work of his intellect and the tendencies of his will. All too soon, and often in an unforeseeable way, what this manifold activity of man yields is not only subjected to "alienation," in the sense that it is simply taken away from the person who produces it, but rather it turns against man himself, at least in part, through the indirect consequences of its effects returning on himself. It is or can be directed against him. This seems to make up the main chapter of the drama of present-day human existence in its broadest and universal dimension.

ENCYCLICAL: THE REDEEMER OF MAN (*Redemptor Hominis*), 1979

John Paul's stand in favor of peace takes no political position. He spoke out against the Shining Path guerrillas in South America as forcefully as against the Iraqi invasion of Kuwait and the American-led war on Iraq. And he has carried his message even to countries actually at war, as he did in Britain during the Falkland Islands war in 1983.

For John Paul one of the tragedies of war-making is its effect on the poor. He has observed that the vast arms arsenals of the world are bought at the cost of depriving the poor of the necessities of life, most evidently in Third World countries, but even in the industrialized West. And extreme poverty itself, in the Holy Father's view, is a grave threat to peace.

The Pope also links peace with religious liberty. He believes that true religious feeling promotes true peace, and that if public authorities ensure religious liberty, they are also furthering the cause of peace. Nor is he unaware that governments are capable of preaching peace and making war simultaneously. Peace, he reminds us, is not a slogan to be used to reassure or to deceive.

John Paul is not a pacifist, and he has said so. He has never denied the necessity to fight war against aggression. But he constantly appeals to warring parties to come together to discuss peace.

The guarantor of peace, in the Holy Father's view, is moral principle, and whatever the social causes of war, personal moral responsibility is central. Without it no peace can last.

PEACE

Peace is not a utopia, nor an inaccessible ideal, nor an unrealizable dream. War is not an inevitable calamity. Peace is possible.

NEGOTIATION: THE ONLY REALISTIC SOLUTION TO THE
CONTINUING THREAT OF WAR, June 1982

The Israeli and Palestinian peoples are already shouldering a burden of suffering which is too heavy. This burden must not be increased; instead it deserves the utmost commitment to finding the paths of necessary and courageous compromises. Efforts in this regard will certainly earn you the gratitude of coming generations and of all humanity. For only a Holy Land at peace will be able to welcome in a worthy manner the thousands of pilgrims who during the Great Jubilee of the Year 2000 will wish to come to pray there.

LETTER TO BENJAMIN NETANYAHU AND YASIR ARAFAT,
June 16, 1997

All people together, Jews, Christians and Muslims, Israelis and Arabs, believers and nonbelievers, must create and reinforce peace; the peace of treaties, the peace of trust, the peace in people's hearts! In this part of the world, as elsewhere, peace cannot be just nor can it long endure unless it rests on sincere dialogue between equal partners, with respect for each other's identity and history, unless it rests on the right of peoples to the free determination of their own destiny, upon their independence and security. There can be no exception! And all those who have accompanied the parties most directly involved in the difficult Middle East peace process must redouble their efforts to ensure that the modest capital of trust already accumulated is not wasted but rather increases and bears interest.

ADDRESS TO THE DIPLOMATIC CORPS, January 13, 1997

Wars, even when they "solve" the problems which cause them, do so only by leaving a wake of victims and destruction which weighs heavily upon ensuing peace negotiations. Awareness of this should encourage peoples, nations and states once and for all to rise above the "culture of war," not only in its most detestable form, namely the power to wage war used as an instrument of supremacy, but also in the less odious but not less destructive form of recourse to arms as an expeditious way to solve a problem. Precisely in a time such as ours, which is familiar with the most sophisticated technologies of destruction, it is urgently necessary to develop a consistent "culture of peace," which will forestall and counter the seemingly inevitable outbreaks of armed violence, including taking steps to stop the growth of the arms industry and of arms trafficking.

MESSAGE FOR WORLD DAY OF THE SICK, 1997, October 18, 1996

Besides the basic education provided by the family, children have a right to a specific training for peace at school and in other educational settings. These institutions have a duty to lead children gradually to understand the nature and demands of peace within their world and culture. Children need to learn the history of peace and not simply the history of victory and defeat in war.

Let us show them examples of peace and not just examples of violence! Fortunately many positive examples of this can be found in every culture and period of history. Suitable new educational opportunities must be created, especially in those situations where cultural and moral poverty has been most oppressive. Everything possible should be done to help children to become messengers of peace.

MESSAGE FOR WORLD DAY OF PEACE, August 8, 1995

Auschwitz, along with so many other concentration camps, remains the horribly eloquent symbol of the effects of totalitarianism. It is our duty to make a pilgrimage to these places, in mind and heart, on their fiftieth anniversary. As I said at the Mass celebrated in 1979 at Brzezinka near Auschwitz: "I kneel at this Golgotha of the modern world." Recalling that pilgrimage, I now go back in spirit to those death camps. I pause especially "before the inscription in Hebrew" which commemorates the people "whose sons and daughters were condemned to total extermination" and reaffirm that "no one is permitted to pass by with indifference."

ADDRESS ON THE FIFTIETH ANNIVERSARY OF THE END OF
WORLD WAR II IN EUROPE, May 8, 1995

The divisions caused by the Second World War make us realize that force in the service of the will to power is an inadequate means for building true justice. Instead, it sets in motion a sinister process with unforeseeable consequences for men, women and whole peoples, who risk the complete loss of their dignity, together with their property and life itself. We can still appreciate the stern warning which Pope Pius XII of venerable memory voiced in August 1939, on the very eve of that tragic conflict, in a last-minute attempt to prevent recourse to arms: "The danger is imminent, but there is yet time. Nothing is lost with peace; all may be lost with war. Let men return to mutual understanding. Let them begin negotiations anew."

ADDRESS ON THE FIFTIETH ANNIVERSARY OF THE END OF
WORLD WAR II IN EUROPE, May 8, 1995

One fact seriously paralyzing the progress of many nations in America is the arms race. The particular Churches in America must raise a prophetic voice to condemn the arms race and the scandalous arms trade, which consumes huge sums of money which should instead be used to combat poverty and promote development.

ECCLESIA IN AMERICA
Post-synodal Apostolic Exhortation, January 22, 1999

The Catholic Church in every place on earth proclaims a message of peace, prays for peace, educates for peace. This purpose is also shared by the representatives and followers of other churches and communities and of other religions of the world, and they have pledged themselves to it. In union with efforts by all people of good will, this work is certainly bearing fruit. Nevertheless, we are continually troubled by the armed conflicts that break out from time to time.

ADDRESS TO THE UNITED NATIONS, October 2, 1979

War is the work of man. War is the destruction of human life. War is death. Nowhere do these truths impose themselves upon us more forcefully than in this city of Hiroshima, at this Peace Memorial.

ADDRESS AT THE PEACE MEMORIAL, HIROSHIMA, February 25, 1981

In current conditions, "deterrence" based on balance, certainly not as an end in itself but as a step on the way toward a progressive disarmament, may still be judged morally acceptable. Nonetheless in order to ensure peace, it is indispensable not to be satisfied with this minimum which is always susceptible to the real danger of explosion.

NEGOTIATION: THE ONLY REALISTIC SOLUTION TO THE
CONTINUING THREAT OF WAR, June 1982

In fact, nuclear weapons are not the only means of war and destruction. The production and sale of conventional weapons throughout the world is a truly alarming and evidently growing phenomenon. No negotiations about armaments would be complete if they were to ignore the fact that 80 percent of the expenditures for weapons are devoted to conventional arms. Moreover, the traffic in these weapons seems to be developing at an increasing rate and seems to be directed most of all toward developing countries. Every step taken to limit this production and traffic and to bring them under an ever more effective control will be an important contribution to the cause of peace.

NEGOTIATION: THE ONLY REALISTIC SOLUTION TO THE
CONTINUING THREAT OF WAR, June 1982

In our modern world to refuse peace means not only to provoke the sufferings and the loss that—today more than ever—war, even a limited one, implies: it could also involve the total destruction of entire regions, not to mention the threat of possible or probable catastrophes in ever vaster and possibly even universal proportions.

NEGOTIATION: THE ONLY REALISTIC SOLUTION TO THE
CONTINUING THREAT OF WAR, June 1982

The ancients said: "*Si vis parem, para bellum*" [If you want peace, prepare for war]. But can our age still really believe that the breathtaking spiral of armaments is at the service of world peace? In alleging the threat of a potential enemy, is it not really rather the intention to keep for oneself a means of threat, in order to get the upper hand with the aid of one's own arsenal of destruction?

Here too it is the human dimension of peace that tends to vanish in favor of ever new possible forms of imperialism.

ADDRESS TO THE UNITED NATIONS, October 2, 1979

The second half of our century, in its turn, brings with it—as though in proportion to the mistakes and transgressions of our contemporary civilization—such a horrible threat of nuclear war that we cannot think of this period except in terms of an incomparable accumulation of sufferings, even to the possible self-destruction of humanity.

APOSTOLIC LETTER ON THE CHRISTIAN MEANING
OF HOLY SUFFERING, 1984

Where there is no justice—who does not know it—there cannot be peace, because injustice is already a disorder and the word of the prophet remains true: "*opus justitia pax*" ("the work of justice is peace," Is 32:17). Likewise, where there is no respect for human rights—I speak of inalienable rights inherent in the person as person—there cannot be peace because every violation of personal dignity favors rancor and the spirit of vendetta.

CHRISTMAS ADDRESS, December 22, 1978

The embargo in particular, clearly defined by law, is an instrument which needs to be used with great discernment, and it must be subjected to strict legal and ethical criteria. It is a means of exerting pressure on governments which have violated the international code of good conduct and of causing them to reconsider their choices. But in a sense it is also an act of force and, as certain cases of the present moment demonstrate, it inflicts grave hardships upon the people of the countries at which it is aimed. I often receive appeals for help from individuals suffering from confinement and extreme poverty. Here I would like to remind you who are diplomats that, before imposing such measures, it is always imperative to foresee the humanitarian consequences of sanctions, without failing to respect the just proportion that such measures should have in relation to the very evil which they are meant to remedy.

AVERTING CIVILIZATION'S RUIN
Address to the Diplomatic Corps, January 19, 1995

We all know well that the areas of misery and hunger on our globe could have been made fertile in a short time, if the gigantic investments for armaments at the service of war and destruction had been changed into investments for food at the service of life.

ENCYCLICAL: THE REDEEMER OF MAN (*Redemptor Hominis*), 1979

The duty of peace falls especially upon the leaders of the world. It is up to the representatives of governments and peoples to work to free humanity not only from wars and conflicts but from the fear that is generated by ever more sophisticated and deadly weapons. Peace is not only the absence of war; it also involves reciprocal trust between nations—a trust that is manifested and proved through constructive negotiations that aim at ending the arms race, and at liberating immense resources that can be used to alleviate misery and feed millions of hungry human beings.

COMMENTS AT MEETING WITH PRESIDENT RONALD REAGAN,
June 7, 1982

To remember Hiroshima is to commit oneself to peace. To remember what the people of this city suffered is to renew our faith in man, in his capacity to do what is good, in his freedom to choose what is right, in his determination to turn disaster into a new beginning. In the face of the man-made calamity that every war is, one must affirm and reaffirm again and again that the waging of war is not inevitable or unchangeable. Humanity is not destined to self-destruction.

ADDRESS AT THE PEACE MEMORIAL, HIROSHIMA,
February 25, 1981

Prayer is a conversation with God, and God's invitation to pray, to converse with Him, is proof of the high esteem in which He holds human beings. John Paul emphasizes strongly the importance of individual dignity in this matter—prayer is an individual speaking directly to God.

In the family, prayer becomes an expression of the family's union with Christ. All the important moments of family life—births and deaths, wedding anniversaries and birthdays, homecomings and departures, important decisions and family crises—should be occasions for prayer. Parents must set an example by praying themselves, and praying with their children.

This private or familial prayer should be the prelude to the liturgical prayer of the Church, and especially to participation in the celebration of the Mass. By observing the liturgical year and its holidays, the family can help to integrate private prayer into the public prayer of the Church. Private prayer is sustained by the ministry of the Church, and especially by the sacraments of penance and Holy Eucharist.

PRAYER

O Virgin Mother,
guide and sustain us
so that we might always live
as true sons and daughters
of the Church of your Son
Enable us to do our part
in helping to establish on earth
the civilization of truth and love,

as God wills it,
for His glory.
Amen.

APOSTOLIC EXHORTATION *Christifedeles Laici,* December 30, 1988

Prayer calls us to examine our consciences on all the issues that affect humanity. It calls us to ponder our personal and collective responsibility before the judgment of God and in the light of human solidarity. Hence prayer is able to transform the world. Everything is new with prayer, both for individuals and for communities. New goals and new ideals emerge. Christian dignity and action are reaffirmed. The commitments of our Baptism, Confirmation and Holy Orders take on new urgency. The horizons of conjugal love and of the mission of the family are vastly extended in prayer.

SPEECH AT ATLANTA, GEORGIA, June 10, 1988

May the perspective of the forthcoming Great Jubilee of the Year 2000 bring about in everyone an attitude of humility, capable of effecting "the necessary purification of past memories" through prayer and conversion of heart, so as to help people to ask and give mutual forgiveness for the misunderstandings of centuries past.

APOSTOLIC LETTER ON THE 350TH ANNIVERSARY OF THE
UKRAINIAN UNION WITH ROME, April 18, 1996

Along the ecumenical path to unity, pride of place certainly belongs to common prayer, the prayerful union of those who gather together around Christ Himself. If Christians, despite their divisions, can grow ever more united in common prayer around Christ, they will grow in the awareness of how little divides them in comparison to what unites them. If they meet more often and more regularly before Christ in prayer, they will be able to gain the courage to face all the painful human reality of their divisions, and they will find themselves together once more in that community of the Church which Christ constantly builds up in the Holy Spirit, in spite of all weaknesses and human limitations.

ENCYCLICAL: THAT ALL MAY BE ONE (*Unum Sint*), 1995

If you really wish to follow Christ, if you want your love for Him to grow and last, then you must be faithful to prayer. It is the key to the vitality of your life in Christ. Without prayer, your faith and love will die. If you are constant in daily prayer and in the Sunday celebration of Mass, your love for Jesus will increase. And your heart will know deep joy and peace.

SPEECH AT NEW ORLEANS, September 12, 1987

When it is difficult therefore to pray, the most important thing is not to stop praying, not to give up the effort. At these times, turn to the Bible and go to the Church's liturgy. Meditate on the life and teachings of Jesus as recorded in the Gospels. Ponder the wisdom and counsel of the Apostles and the challenging messages of the Prophets. Try to make your own the beautiful prayers of the Psalms. You will find in the inspired word of God the spiritual food you need. Above all, your soul will be refreshed when you take part wholeheartedly with the community in the celebration of the Eucharist, the Church's greatest prayer.

SPEECH AT NEW ORLEANS, September 12, 1987

Through the prayer of Christ to which we give voice, our day is sanctified, our activities transformed, our actions made holy. We pray the same psalms that Jesus prayed and come into personal contact with Him—the person to whom all Scripture points, the goal to which all history is directed.

SPEECH AT ST. PATRICK'S CATHEDRAL, NEW YORK CITY,
October 3, 1979

It is significant that precisely in and through prayer man comes to discover in a very simple and yet profound way his own unique subjectivity: In prayer the human "I" more easily perceives the depth of what it means to be a person.

LETTER TO FAMILIES FOR THE INTERNATIONAL YEAR
OF THE FAMILY, February 22, 1994

Prayer increases the strength and spiritual unity of the family, helping the family to partake of God's own "strength."

LETTER TO FAMILIES FOR THE INTERNATIONAL YEAR
OF THE FAMILY, February 22, 1994

There are several definitions of prayer. But it is most often called a talk, a conversation, a colloquy with God. Conversing with someone, not only do we speak but we also listen. Prayer, therefore, is also listening. It consists of listening to hear the interior voice of grace. Listening to hear the call. And then, as you ask me how the Pope prays, I answer you: like every Christian—he speaks and he listens. Sometimes, he prays without words, and then he listens all the more. The most important thing is precisely what he "hears." And he also tries to unite prayer with his obligations, his activities, his work, and to unite his work with prayer. In this way, day after day, he tries to carry out his "service," his "ministry," which comes to him from the will of Christ and from the living tradition of the Church.

ADDRESS TO THE INSTITUT CATHOLIQUE, PARIS,
June 1, 1980

Prayer can truly change your life. For it turns your attention away from yourself and directs your mind and your heart toward the Lord. If we look only at ourselves, with our own limitations and sins, we quickly give way to sadness and discouragement. But if we keep our eyes fixed on the Lord, then our hearts are filled with hope, our minds are washed in the light of truth and we come to know the fullness of the Gospel with all its promise and life.

ADDRESS TO YOUTH AT NEW ORLEANS, September 12, 1987

Only a worshiping and praying Church can show herself sufficiently sensitive to the needs of the sick, the suffering, the lonely—especially in the great urban centers—and the poor everywhere. The Church as a community of service has first to feel the weight of the burden carried by so many individuals and families, and then strive to help alleviate these burdens. The discipleship that the Church discovers in prayer she expresses in deep interest for Christ's brethren in the modern world and for their many different needs. Her concern, manifested in various ways, embraces—among others—the areas of housing, education, health care, unemployment, the administration of justice, the special needs of the aged and the handicapped. In prayer, the Church is confirmed in her solidarity with the weak who are oppressed, the vulnerable who are manipulated, the children who are exploited and everyone who is in any way discriminated against.

Ad Limina ADDRESS TO U.S. BISHOPS, December 3, 1983

The universal Church of Christ, and therefore each particular Church, exists in order to pray. In prayer the human person expresses his or her nature; the community expresses its vocation; the Church reaches out to God. In prayer the Church attains fellowship with the Father and with His Son, Jesus Christ (see 1 Jn 1:3). In prayer the Church expresses her Trinitarian life, because she directs herself to the Father, undergoes the action of the Holy Spirit and lives fully her relationship with Christ. Indeed, she experiences herself as the Body of Christ, and the mystical Christ.

ADDRESS TO BISHOPS AT ATLANTA, June 10, 1988

It should never be forgotten that prayer constitutes an essential part of Christian life, understood in its fullness and centrality. Indeed, prayer is an important part of our very humanity: it is "the first expression of man's inner truth, the first condition for authentic freedom of spirit."

APOSTOLIC EXHORTATION *Familiari Consortio,* 1981

Family prayer has for its very own object family life itself, which in all its varying circumstances is seen as a call from God and lived as a filial response to His call. Joys and sorrows, hopes and disappointments, births and birthday celebrations, wedding anniversaries of the parents, departures, separations and home-comings, important and far-reaching decisions, the death of those who are dear, etc.—all of these mark God's loving intervention in the family's history. They should be seen as suitable moments for thanksgiving, for petition, for trusting abandonment of the family into the hands of their common Father in heaven.

APOSTOLIC EXHORTATION *Familiaris Consortio,* 1981

The truth of prayer is both the cause and effect of a lifestyle which is placed in the light of the Gospel.

MESSAGE FOR WORLD MISSION DAY, October 18, 1981

In light of this difficulty we must demonstrate incessantly that Christian prayer is inseparable from our faith in God, Father, Son and Holy Spirit, from our faith in His love and His redeeming power, which is at work in the world. Therefore, prayer is worth-while above all for us: Lord, "increase our faith" (Lk 17:6). It has as its goal our conversion, that is, as St. Cyprian explained, inte-rior and exterior openness, the will to open oneself to the trans-forming action of grace.

MESSAGE FOR WORLD MISSION DAY, October 18, 1981

The rosary is my favorite prayer. A marvelous prayer! Marvelous in its simplicity and in its depth. In the prayer we repeat many times the words that the Virgin Mary heard from the Archangel, and from her kinswoman Elizabeth.

VATICAN ADDRESS, October 26, 1978

O Divine Master, grant that I may not so much seek to be con-soled as to console, to be understood as to understand, to be loved as to love; for it is in giving that we receive, it is in pardoning that we are pardoned, and it is in dying that we are born to eternal life.

PRAYER OF ST. FRANCIS OF ASSISI,
Speech to Interreligious Leaders at Los Angeles, September 16, 1987

The search for scientific truth is extremely important to this highly intellectual and scientifically minded Pope. To the Holy Father, applying reason to nature is a worthy pursuit, and the products of such work are a positive good. Science has great potential as a unifying force and thus creates no conflict with religion. In fact, scientific progress serves spiritual progress, because through science and technology we free ourselves to pursue good works and service to others.

John Paul has urged theologians to eliminate scientific ignorance by entering into a meaningful dialogue with scientists. When he remarked in 1979 that "Galileo suffered greatly at the hands of churchmen," he was referring to an ignorance of science. He urges theologians and scientists alike to "be aware of our own competencies" and always to be faithful to the truth, because "the truth shall make you free."

Furthermore, scientists, who study the body merely as a machine, achieve an impressive but nevertheless limited truth and understanding: The human body has a spiritual component, which cannot be ignored or denied.

John Paul calls upon scientists to take responsibility for their research, particularly in the areas of genetics and nuclear science, the first because it may allow a person to be converted into a means rather than respected as an individual, and the second because it can, in certain applications, threaten continued life on earth.

Far from opposing development, John Paul sees underdevelopment as a source of injustice, poverty, and war. When he criticizes the material preoccupations of rich countries, it is not because he is interested in slowing progress but because he believes that where the search for increasing material wealth dominates, there can be no real progress. True progress requires not only the satisfaction of material needs but the achievement of spiritual fulfillment as well.

Progress and the Modern World

The dominion granted to man by the Creator is not an absolute power, nor can one speak of a freedom to "use and misuse," or to dispose of things as one pleases. The limitation imposed from the beginning by the Creator Himself and expressed symbolically by the prohibition not to "eat of the fruit of the tree" (cf. Gen 2:16–17) shows clearly enough that, when it comes to the natural world, we are subject not only to biological laws but also to moral ones, which cannot be violated with impunity.

ENCYCLICAL: ON SOCIAL CONCERNS (*Sollicitudo Rei Socialis*), 1987

Any progress which would secure the betterment of a select few at the expense of the greater human family would be an erroneous and distorted progress. It would be an outrage against the demands of justice and an affront to the dignity of every human being.

BUILDING UP THE BODY OF CHRIST
Pastoral Visit to the United States, 1987

In the secularized modern age we are seeing the emergence of a twofold temptation: a concept of knowledge no longer understood as wisdom and contemplation, but as power over nature, which is consequently regarded as an object to be conquered. The other temptation is the unbridled exploitation of resources under the urge of unlimited profit-seeking, according to the capitalistic mentality typical of modern societies. Thus the environment has often fallen prey to the interests of a few strong industrial groups, to the detriment of humanity as a whole, with the ensuing damage to the balance of the ecosystem, the health of the inhabitants and of future generations to come.

ADDRESS TO A CONVENTION ON THE ENVIRONMENT
AND HEALTH, March 24, 1997

I therefore appeal to the conscience of the world's scientific authorities and in particular to doctors, that the production of human embryos be halted, taking into account that there seems to be no morally licit solution regarding the human density of the thousands and thousands of "frozen" embryos which are and remain the subjects of essential rights and should therefore be protected by law as human persons. I also call on all jurists to work so that states and international institutions will legally recognize the natural rights of the very origin of human life and will likewise defend the inalienable rights which these thousands of "frozen" embryos have intrinsically acquired from the moment of fertilization.

ADDRESS AT A SYMPOSIUM ON EVANGELISM, May 24, 1996

Society is more eroticized in an artificial way. Many texts for sex education become an apologia for even the most deviant kinds of behavior. Therefore, the need arises to correct and discipline, and to defend oneself, even with rigorous and puritanical expressions. It is as if the dikes were foolishly destroyed, and then an attempt were made to halt the disaster and divert the raging currents back to their natural channel.

GUIDELINES FOR SEXUAL EDUCATION FOR THE FAMILY,
February 14, 1996

Through the knowledge of genetics and molecular biology, scientists can look with the penetrating gaze of science into the inner fabric of life and the mechanisms that characterize individuals, thus ensuring the continuity of living species. These advances increasingly reveal the Creator's greatness, because they allow man to discover the intrinsic order of creation and to appreciate the wonders of his body, in addition to his intellect, which to a certain extent reflects the light of the Word through whom "all things were made" (Jn 1:3).

DIGNITY OF THE HUMAN GENOME
Address at the Fourth General Assembly of the Pontifical Academy
for Life, February 24, 1998

In the modern era . . . there is a strong tendency to seek knowledge not so much for admiring and contemplating, as for increas-

surely her greatest wealth. This is the time to start out on the new paths called for by the times of renewal which we are experiencing at the approach of the third millennium of the Christian era.

THE DOCTRINE OF FREEDOM AND SOLIDARITY
Homily at the Mass in Havana's Revolution Plaza, January 25, 1998

Should the extension of the human species be desired, this duplication of body structure does not necessarily imply a perfectly identical person, understood in his ontological and psychological reality. The spiritual soul, which is created directly by God, cannot be generated by the parents, produced by artificial insemination or cloned.

HUMAN CLONING IS IMMORAL
Reflections from the Pontifical Academy for Life, July 9, 1997

Halting the human cloning project is a moral duty which must also be translated into cultural, social and legislative terms. The progress of scientific research is not the same as the rise of scientific despotism.

HUMAN CLONING IS IMMORAL
Reflections from the Pontifical Academy for Life, July 9, 1997

The fetal therapies now emerging in the medical, surgical and genetic fields offer new hope of saving the lives of those suffering from pathologies that are either incurable or very difficult to treat after birth. They thus confirm the teaching that the Church has upheld on the basis of both philosophy and theology. Faith, in fact, does not diminish the value and validity of reason; on the contrary, faith sustains and illuminates reason, especially when human weakness or negative psychosocial influences lessen its perspicacity.

THE ETHICS OF FETAL THERAPY
Address to the International Congress The Fetus as a Patient,
April 3, 2000

It is the ecological question—ranging from the preservation of the natural habitats of the different species of animals and of other forms of life to human ecology properly speaking—which

ing power over things. Knowledge and power are interwov
more and more in a mentality that can imprison man himse
With regard to knowledge of the human genome, this mental
could lead to interference with the internal structure of huma
life itself with a view to subduing, selecting and manipulating tl
body and, ultimately, the person and future generations.

DIGNITY OF THE HUMAN GENOM
Address at the Fourth General Assembly of the Pontifical Academ
for Life, February 24, 199

I feel an obligation here to express my concern over the spread of
a cultural climate which is steering prenatal diagnosis in a direction that is no longer one of treatment for the sake of better
accepting the life of the unborn, but rather one of discrimination
against those who do not prove healthy in prenatal examination.
At the current time there is a serious disproportion between diag-
nostic possibilities, which are progressively expanding, and therapeutic possibilities, which are scarce: this fact raises serious ethical
problems for families, who need to be supported in welcoming
newborn life, even when it suffers from some defect or malfor-
mation.

DIGNITY OF THE HUMAN GENOME
Address at the Fourth General Assembly of the Pontifical Academy
for Life, February 24, 1998

The original separation of Church and state in the United States
was certainly not an effort to ban all religious conviction from the
public sphere, a kind of banishment of God from civil society.
Indeed, the vast majority of Americans, regardless of their religious persuasion, are convinced that religious conviction and reli-
giously informed moral argument have a vital role in public life.

THE CHALLENGE TO AMERICAN DEMOCRACY
Address to Mrs. Corinne "Lindy" Boggs, Ambassador of the United
States of America, December 16, 1997

As everyone knows, Cuba has a Christian soul and this has
brought her a universal vocation. Called to overcome isolation,
she needs to open herself to the world and the world needs to
draw close to Cuba, her people, her sons and daughters who are

finds in the Bible clear and strong ethical direction leading to a solution which respects the great good of life, of every life. In fact, the dominion granted to man by the Creator is not an absolute power, nor can one speak of a freedom to "use and misuse," or to dispose of things as one pleases.

ENCYCLICAL: THE GOSPEL OF LIFE (*Evangelium Vitae*), 1994

An ever increasing number of scientists are becoming aware of their human responsibility and are convinced that there cannot be science without conscience. This fundamental thought is a positive and encouraging gain of our own time, which is better able to measure the limits of scientism, which one should take good care not to identify with science itself.

ADDRESS AT THE UNIVERSITY OF FRIBOURG, SWITZERLAND,
June 13, 1984

The various techniques of artificial reproduction, which would seem to be at the service of life and which are frequently used with this intention, actually open the door to new threats against life. . . . The number of embryos produced is often greater than that needed for implantation in the woman's womb, and these so-called spare embryos are then destroyed or used for research which, under the pretext of scientific or medical progress, in fact reduces human life to the level of simple "biological material" to be freely disposed of.

ENCYCLICAL: THE GOSPEL OF LIFE (*Evangelium Vitae*), 1994

We must convince ourselves of the priority of ethics over technology, of the primacy of person over things, of the superiority of spirit over matter (cf. *Redemptor Hominis,* The Redeemer of Man, no. 16).

THE FREEDOM OF CONSCIENCE AND RELIGIONS,
September 1, 1980

It [technology] facilitates his [man's] work, perfects, accelerates and augments it. It leads to an increase in the quantity of things produced by work, and in many cases improves their quality. However, it is also a fact that in some instances technology can cease to be man's ally and become almost his enemy, as when the mechanization of work "supplants" him, taking away all personal satisfaction and the incentive to creativity and responsibility.

ENCYCLICAL: ON HUMAN WORK (*Laborem Exercens*), 1981

Surely we must be grateful for the new technology which enables us to store information in vast man-made artificial memories, thus providing wide and instant access to the knowledge which is our human heritage, to the Church's teaching and tradition, the words of Sacred Scripture, the counsels of the great masters of spirituality, the history and traditions of the local churches, of religious orders and lay institutes, and to the ideas and experiences of initiators and innovators whose insights bear constant witness to the faithful presence in our midst of a loving Father who brings out of His treasure new things and old.

THE CHURCH MUST LEARN TO COPE

WITH THE COMPUTER CULTURE

Statement on World Communication Day, May 27, 1989

[Modern man's] science in the field of biophysiology and biomedicine has made great progress. However, this science deals with man under a determined "aspect" and so is practical rather than global. We know well the functions connected with the masculinity and femininity of the human person, but this science does not yet develop the awareness of the body as a sign of the person, as a manifestation of the spirit.

BLESSED ARE THE PURE OF HEART

General Audience, April 8, 1981

Our period and the periods that preceded it too easily believed that scientific and technological conquests would be the equivalent, or at least the guarantee, of human progress, which progress would bring about freedom and happiness. In our own day, many scholars as well as an increasing number of our contemporaries are realizing that the rash transformation of the world risks jeopardizing in a grave way the complex and delicate equilibrium that exists in nature.

ADDRESS AT THE UNIVERSITY OF FRIBOURG, SWITZERLAND,

June 13, 1984

With the advent of computer telecommunications and what are known as computer participation systems, the Church is offered further means for fulfilling her mission. Methods of facilitating communication and dialogue among her own members can strengthen the bonds of unity between them. Immediate access to information makes it possible for her to deepen her dialogue with the contemporary world.

THE CHURCH MUST LEARN TO COPE
WITH THE COMPUTER CULTURE
Statement on World Communication Day, May 27, 1989

Today we are concerned to see the desert expanding to lands which only yesterday were prosperous and fertile. We cannot forget that in many cases man himself has been the cause of the barrenness of lands which have become desert, just as he has caused the pollution of formerly clean waters. When people do not respect the goods of the earth, when they abuse them, they act unjustly, even criminally, because for many of their brothers and sisters their actions result in poverty and death.

THE WORLD'S EXPANDING DESERTS
Lenten Message, January 7, 1993

Many times in recent years, the Church has addressed issues related to the advances in biomedical technology. She does so not in order to discourage scientific progress or to judge harshly those who seek to extend the frontiers of human knowledge and skill, but in order to affirm the moral truths which must guide the application of this knowledge and skill. Ultimately, the purpose of the Church's teaching in this field is to defend the innate dignity and fundamental rights of the human person. In this regard the Church cannot fail to emphasize the need to safeguard the life and integrity of the human embryo and fetus.

ADDRESS AT PHOENIX, September 14, 1987

The penchant for empirical observation, the procedures of scientific objectification, technological progress and certain forms of liberalism have led to these two terms being set in opposition, as if a dialectic, if not an absolute conflict, between freedom and nature were characteristic of the structure of human history. At other periods, it seemed that "nature" subjected man totally to its own dynamics and even its own unbreakable laws. Today too, the situation of the world of the senses within space and time, physico-chemical constants, bodily processes, psychological impulses and forms of social conditioning seem to many people the only really decisive factors of human reality. In this context even moral facts, despite their specificity, are frequently treated as if they were statistically verifiable data, patterns of behavior which can be subject to observation or explained exclusively in categories of psychosocial processes.

ENCYCLICAL: THE SPLENDOR OF TRUTH (*Veritatis Splendor*), 1993

The prospect of growing economic progress, and the chance of obtaining a greater share of the goods that modern society has to offer, will appear to you as an opportunity to achieve greater freedom. The more you possess—you may be tempted to think—the more you will feel liberated from every type of confinement. In order to make more money and to possess more, in order to eliminate effort and worry, you may be tempted to take moral shortcuts where honesty, truth and work are concerned. The progress of science and technology seems inevitable and you may be enticed to look towards the technological society for the answers to all your problems.

ADDRESS AT DUBLIN, September 29, 1979

Scientific and technological progress, which contemporary man is continually expanding in his dominion over nature, not only offers the hope of creating new and better humanity, but also causes ever-greater anxiety regarding the future. Some ask themselves if it is a good thing to be alive or if it would be better never to have been born; they doubt therefore if it is right to bring others into life when perhaps they will curse their existence in a cruel world with unforeseeable terrors. Others consider themselves to be the only ones for whom the advantages of technology are intended, and they exclude others by imposing on them contraceptives or even worse means. Still others imprisoned in a consumer mentality and whose sole concern is to bring about a continual growth of material goods, finish by ceasing to understand, and thus by refusing, the spiritual riches of a new human life. The ultimate reason for these mentalities is the absence in people's hearts of God, whose love alone is stronger than all the world's fears and can conquer them.

APOSTOLIC EXHORTATION *Familiaris Consortio,* 1981

Perhaps John Paul's most memorable words on the responsibility of the rich to the poor were spoken at Yankee Stadium in 1979, when he urged rich countries, such as the United States, to treat the poor "like guests at your family table," not leaving them merely "the crumbs from the feast" but having them take part in the substance of the meal. Equitable distribution of the world's material bounty has been his constant plea and his consistent concern.

John Paul ties spiritual freedom and freedom from material want closely together. Where extreme poverty dominates, spiritual values collapse and violence flourishes. In this sense, both material and spiritual goods are unequally distributed in the world, and this imbalance must be adjusted.

John Paul is impatient with those who passively notice and pity the poor. Love for the poor, in his view, has to result in deeds. The poor cannot be ignored with the justification that there is a better world awaiting them. Individuals with great riches must share them; families with two incomes must share with those who have none; nations blessed with ample material wealth must share it with those that have little. The Holy Father urges that all have "a special preference" for the poor and the hungry, not just a passive concern.

The Pope can be very specific about what a "special preference" for the poor means, particularly regarding the redistribution of wealth. He has not hesitated to embrace the poor, even the revolutionary poor, in their fight against the evil of poverty.

RICH AND POOR

If you only want to have more and more, if your idol is profit and pleasure, remember that man's value is not measured by what he has, but by what he is. So let him who has accumulated a great deal, and who thinks that everything is summed up in this, remember that he may be worth far less (within himself and in the eyes of God) than any of those poor and unknown persons.

ADDRESS TO INDIANS OF AMAZONIA, June 30, 1980

One of the greatest injustices in the contemporary world consists precisely in this: that the ones who possess much are relatively few and those who possess almost nothing are many. It is the injustice of the poor distribution of the goods and services originally intended for all.

ENCYCLICAL: ON SOCIAL CONCERNS (*Sollicitudo Rei Socialis*), 1987

As I mentioned earlier, the complex phenomenon of globalization is one of the features of the contemporary world particularly visible in America. An important part of this many-faceted reality is the economic aspect. By her social doctrine, the Church makes an effective contribution to the issues presented by the current globalized economy. Her moral vision in this area rests on the threefold cornerstone of human dignity, solidarity and subsidiarity. The globalized economy must be analyzed in the light of the principles of social justice, respecting the preferential option for the poor, who must be allowed to take their place in such an economy, and the requirements of the international common good.

ECCLESIA IN AMERICA
Post-synodal Apostolic Exhortation, January 22, 1999

It is not right for anyone—still less for public authorities responsible for the common good—to disregard the tragic situation of so many individuals and entire families forced to live on the street or to be content with inhospitable, makeshift shelters. It is also said that so many young people, because of the difficulty in finding housing, often due to the lack or uncertainty of work, must postpone their marriage for a long time or even forgo the starting of their own family. Therefore, may this renewed expression of the international ethical and juridical conscience enjoy success: as it confirms the right to housing for all, it also stresses the close connection of this right with the right to start a family and to have an adequately paid job.

ADDRESS TO THE UN CONFERENCE ON HUMAN SETTLEMENTS,
June 16, 1996

One of the most bitter fruits of wars and economic hardships is the sad phenomenon of refugees and displaced persons, a phenomenon which, as the synod mentioned, has reached tragic dimensions. The ideal solution is the reestablishment of a just peace, reconciliation and economic development. It is therefore urgent that national, regional and international organizations should find equable and long-lasting solutions to the problems of refugees and displaced persons. In the meantime, since the continent continues to suffer from the massive displacement of refugees, I make a pressing appeal that these people be given material help and offered pastoral support wherever they may be, whether in Africa or on other continents.

ADDRESS DURING PASTORAL VISIT TO AFRICA,
September 14, 1995

There are many reasons for this paradoxical situation in which abundance coexists with scarcity, including policies which forcibly reduce agricultural production, widespread corruption in public life and massive investment in sophisticated weapons systems to the detriment of people's primary needs. These and other reasons contribute to the creation of what you call "structures of famine." Here we are speaking of the mechanisms of international business by which the less favored countries, those most in need of food, are excluded in one way or another from the market, thus preventing a just and effective distribution of agricultural products. Yet another reason is that certain forms of assistance for development are made conditional on the implementation by poorer countries of policies of structural adjustment, policies which drastically limit those countries' ability to acquire needed foodstuffs.

ADDRESS TO THE TWENTY-EIGHTH CONFERENCE OF THE U.N.
FOOD AND AGRICULTURAL ORGANIZATION, October 23, 1995

The equitable distribution of goods, desired by the Creator, is also an urgent imperative in the area of health: the persistent injustice that deprives a large part of the population of the treatment indispensable to health, especially in poor countries, must cease once and for all. This is a grave scandal which can only prompt national leaders to make every effort to ensure that those who lack material means are provided with access to at least basic health care. Promoting "health for all" is a primary duty for every member of the international community; for Christians it is a commitment closely connected with their witness of faith.

MESSAGE FOR WORLD DAY OF THE SICK, 2001, August 22, 2000

This is the scandal of the affluent society of today's world, in which the rich grow ever richer, since wealth produces wealth, and the poor grow ever poorer, since poverty tends to additional poverty. Not only is this scandal found within individual nations, but it also has aspects which extend well beyond their borders. Today, especially, with the phenomenon of the globalization of markets, the rich and developed nations tend to improve their economic status further, while the poor countries—with the exception of some in the process of a promising development—tend to sink into ever more grievous forms of poverty.

ADDRESS AT THE JUBILEE OF GOVERNMENT LEADERS, MEMBERS
OF PARLIAMENT, AND POLITICIANS, November 4, 2000

When large landholdings are insufficiently used, this justifies expropriation of land—with adequate compensation to the owners—so that it can be allocated to those who have none or not enough.

TOWARDS A BETTER DISTRIBUTION OF LAND
Document of the Pontifical Council for Justice and Peace on the
Challenge of Agrarian Reform, November 23, 1997

Even though the international debt is not the sole cause of poverty in many developing countries, it cannot be denied that it has contributed to creating conditions of extreme privation which constitute an urgent challenge to the conscience of humankind.

ENCOUNTER WITH JESUS: CONVERSIONS, COMMUNION AND
SOLIDARITY
Message of the Special Assembly for America of the Synod of Bishops,
December 9, 1997

Relief from debt will only begin to lift the burdens of the poor. Much more will have to be done to prevent the marginalization of whole countries and regions from the global economy. Any reduction of the debt must truly result in benefit to the poor. Measures must be taken to avoid the causes—whatever they may be—that created the debt.

ENCOUNTER WITH JESUS: CONVERSIONS, COMMUNION AND
SOLIDARITY
Message of the Special Assembly for America of the Synod of Bishops,
December 9, 1997

In light of the imminent Great Jubilee of the Year 2000, and recalling the social significance that jubilees had in the Old Testament, I wrote: "In the spirit of the Book of Leviticus (25:8–12), Christians will have to raise their voice on behalf of all the poor of the world, proposing the jubilee as an appropriate time to give thought, among other things, to reducing substantially, if not canceling outright, the international debt which seriously threatens the future of many nations."

ECCLESIA IN AMERICA
Post-synodal Apostolic Exhortation, January 22, 1999

Surmounting every type of imperialism and determination to preserve their own hegemony, the stronger and richer nations must have a sense of moral responsibility for the other nations, so that a real international system may be established which will rest on the foundation of the equality of all peoples and on the necessary respect for their legitimate differences. The economically weaker countries, or those still at subsistence level, must be enabled, with the assistance of other peoples and of the international community, to make a contribution of their own to the common good with their treasures of humanity and culture, which otherwise would be lost forever.

ENCYCLICAL: ON SOCIAL CONCERNS (*Sollicitudo Rei Socialis*), 1987

But the person who, like the rich landowner in the Gospel parable, thinks that he can make his life secure by the possession of material goods alone is deluding himself. Life is slipping away from him, and very soon he will find himself bereft of it without ever having appreciated its real meaning: "Fool! This night your soul is required of you; and the things you have prepared, whose will they be?" (Lk 12:20).

ENCYCLICAL: THE GOSPEL OF LIFE (*Evangelium Vitae*), 1994

A disconcerting conclusion about the most recent period should serve to enlighten us: side-by-side with the miseries of underdevelopment, themselves unacceptable, we find ourselves up against a form of superdevelopment, equally inadmissible, because like the former it is contrary to what is good and to true happiness. This superdevelopment, which consists in an excessive availability of every kind of material goods for the benefit of certain social groups, easily makes people slaves of "possession" and of immediate gratification, with no other horizon than the multiplication or continual replacement of the things already owned with others still better. This is the so-called civilization of consumption or consumerism, which involves so much "throwing-away" and "waste."

ENCYCLICAL: ON SOCIAL CONCERNS (*Sollicitudo Rei Socialis*), 1987

When the West gives the impression of abandoning itself to forms of growing and selfish isolation, and the East in its turn seems to ignore for questionable reasons its duty to cooperate in the task of alleviating human misery, then we are up against not only a betrayal of humanity's legitimate expectations—a betrayal that is a harbinger of unforeseeable consequences—but also a real desertion of a moral obligation.

ENCYCLICAL: ON SOCIAL CONCERNS (*Sollicitudo Rei Socialis*), 1987

In such a context, in which new forms of poverty emerge, the homeless make up a group that is still poorer than the poor; all of us need to help them. We are convinced that a house is much more than a simple roof over one's head. The place where a person creates and lives out his or her life also serves to found, in some way, that person's deepest identity and his or her relations with others.

NEGOTIATION: THE ONLY REALISTIC SOLUTION TO THE CONTINUING THREAT OF WAR, June 1982

Social thinking and social practice inspired by the Gospel must always be marked by a special sensitivity toward those who are most in distress, those who are extremely poor, those suffering from all the physical, mental and moral ills that afflict humanity, including hunger, neglect, unemployment and despair.

HOMILY AT MASS AT YANKEE STADIUM,
NEW YORK, October 2, 1979

Without going into an analysis of figures and statistics, it is sufficient to face squarely the reality of an innumerable multitude of people—children, adults and the elderly—in other words, real and unique human persons, who are suffering under the intolerable burden of poverty.

ENCYCLICAL: ON SOCIAL CONCERNS (*Sollicitudo Rei Socialis*), 1987

The poor of the United States and of the world are your brothers and sisters in Christ. You must never be content to leave them just the crumbs from the feast. You must take of your substance, and not just of your abundance, in order to help them. And you must treat them like guests at your family table.

HOMILY AT MASS AT YANKEE STADIUM,
NEW YORK, October 2, 1979

Recall the time when Jesus saw the hungry crowd gathered on the hillside. What was his response? He did not content himself with expressing his compassion. He gave his disciples the command "Give them something to eat yourselves" [Mt 14:16]. Did he not intend those same words for us today, for us who live at the closing of the twentieth century, for us who have the means available to feed the hungry of the world?

ADDRESS AT DES MOINES, IOWA, October 4, 1979

In the light of Christ's words, this poor South will judge the rich North. And the poor people and poor nations—poor in different ways, not only lacking food, but also deprived of freedom and other human rights—will judge those people who take these goods away from them, amassing to themselves the imperialistic monopoly of economic and political supremacy at the expense of others.

HOMILY AT MASS AT EDMONTON, ALBERTA, September 17, 1984

Even in this wealthy nation, committed by its founding fathers to the dignity and equality of all persons, the black community suffers a disproportionate share of economic deprivation. Far too many of our young people receive less than an equal opportunity for a quality education and for gainful employment. The Church must continue to join her effort with the efforts of others who are working to correct all imbalances and disorders of a social nature. Indeed, the Church can never remain silent in the face of injustice wherever it is clearly present.

ADDRESS AT NEW ORLEANS, September 12, 1987

The number of people living in extreme poverty is enormous. I am thinking, for example, of the tragic situations in certain countries of Africa, Asia and Latin America. There exist vast groups, often whole sectors of the population, which find themselves on the margins of civil life within their own countries. Among them is a growing number of children who in order to survive can rely on nobody except themselves. Such a situation is not only an affront to human dignity but also represents a clear threat to peace. A state, whatever its political organization or economic system, remains fragile and unstable if it does not give constant attention to its weakest members and if it fails to do everything possible to ensure that at least their primary needs are satisfied.

THE LINKS BETWEEN POVERTY AND PEACE
Message for World Day of Peace 1993, December 11, 1992

In the interest of the individual—and thus of peace—it is therefore urgently necessary to introduce into the mechanisms of the economy the necessary correctives which will enable the mechanisms to ensure a more just and equitable distribution of goods. By itself the rules of the market are not sufficient to accomplish this; society must accept its own responsibilities. It must do so by increasing its efforts, which are often already considerable, to eliminate the causes of poverty and their tragic consequences. No country by itself can succeed in such an undertaking. For this very reason it is necessary to work together, with that solidarity demanded by a world which has become ever more interdependent. To allow situations of extreme poverty to persist is to create social conditions ever more exposed to the threat of violence and conflict.

THE LINKS BETWEEN POVERTY AND PEACE
Message for World Day of Peace, 1993, December 11, 1992

Development cannot consist only in the use, dominion over and indiscriminate possession of created things and the products of human industry, but rather in subordinating the possessions, dominion and the use to man's divine likeness and to his vocation to immortality.

ENCYCLICAL: ON SOCIAL CONCERNS (*Sollicitudo Rei Socialis*), 1987

In the final analysis, however, we must realize that social injustice and unjust social structures exist only because individuals and groups of individuals deliberately maintain or tolerate them. It is these personal choices, operating through structures, that breed and propagate situations of poverty, oppression and misery. For this reason, overcoming "social" sin and reforming the social order itself must begin with the conversion of our hearts. As the American bishops have said: "The Gospel confers on each Christian the vocation to love God and neighbor in ways that bear fruit in the life of society. That vocation consists above all in a change of heart: a conversion expressed in praise of God and in concrete deeds of justice and service."

ECONOMIC JUSTICE FOR ALL: CATHOLIC SOCIAL TEACHING AND
THE U.S. ECONOMY
Address to Catholic Charities, California, September 19, 1987

Christ's death on the cross unites physical and spiritual suffering: He took upon Himself the moral evil of sin and suffered for that.

John Paul has himself suffered considerable physical pain, both in his younger years and more recently. The wound he suffered in the attempt on his life is well known; hospital stays in recent years for various ailments have been terribly painful for him. He has an almost mystical vision of himself as suffering for all mankind. From his hospital bed in May 1994, he referred to his present physical pain and to the attempt on his life more than a decade before as evidence that the Pope must suffer, in a sense taking on the pain that others suffer.

John Paul emphasizes that in the face of the suffering of others, compassion and sympathy, however heartfelt, are not enough. Action to relieve suffering is the only moral course, an obligation that cannot be evaded. On the other hand, suffering can transform us, teach us compassion, and so draw us closer to Christ. Through suffering we—as did He—take part in saving the world. Thus "in our sufferings we find inner peace and even spiritual joy."

The Pope has spoken often of the suffering of the elderly, including not only their physical discomforts but also their emotional and psychological pain. The family, John Paul always insists, is the source of relief from this pain.

Finally, the Holy Father reminds those facing death of their participation in the death and resurrection of the Lord, that prayer is the source of hope in times of crisis, and that no pain and suffering is greater than that of the spiritual separation from God.

SUFFERING, DYING, AND DEATH

Sacred Scripture is a great book about suffering.

APOSTOLIC LETTER ON THE CHRISTIAN MEANING
OF HOLY SUFFERING, 1984

All concern for the sick and suffering is part of the Church's life and mission. The Church has always understood itself to be charged by Christ with the care of the poor, the weak, the defenseless, the suffering and those who mourn. This means that as you alleviate suffering and seek to heal, you also bear witness to the Christian view of suffering and to the meaning of life and death as taught by your Christian faith.

HOMILY AT MASS IN LOS ANGELES COLISEUM, September 15, 1987

The Letter to the Hebrews also speaks of being made perfect through suffering (see Heb 5:8–10). This is because the purifying flames of trial and sorrow have the power to transform us from within by unleashing our love, teaching us compassion for others, and thus drawing us closer to Christ. Next to her Son, Mary is the most perfect example of this. It is precisely in being the Mother of Sorrows that she is a mother to each one of us and to all of us. The spiritual sword that pierces her heart opens up a river of compassion for all who suffer.

HOMILY AT MASS IN LOS ANGELES COLISEUM, September 15, 1987

Dear brothers and sisters who are suffering in spirit and in body! Do not yield to the temptation to regard pain as an experience which is only negative, to the point of doubting God's goodness. In the suffering Christ every sick person finds the meaning of his or her afflictions. Suffering and illness belong to the condition of man, a fragile, limited creature, marked by original sin from birth. In Christ, who died and rose again, however, humanity discovers a new dimension to its suffering: instead of a failure, it reveals itself to be the occasion for offering witness to faith and love.

MESSAGE FOR WORLD DAY OF THE SICK, 1997, October 18, 1996

At a time like ours, in which man is able to bend even the laws of nature to his will, drug addiction with its capacity for damaging the person's will power is an obstacle that reveals the intimate fragility of the human being and his need for help from the world that surrounds him and, even more radically, from Him who alone can act in the depth of his psyche in difficulty. The relationship with God, lived in an attitude of authentic faith, is an extraordinarily effective support on the journey to recovery from humanly desperate situations. Those who have experienced this know it well and can testify to it.

ADDRESS TO THE ITALIAN FEDERATION OF THERAPEUTIC
COMMUNITIES, June 26, 1995

In this spirit, dear elderly brothers and sisters, as I encourage each of you to live with serenity the years that the Lord has granted you, I feel a spontaneous desire to share fully with you my own feelings at this point of my life, after more than twenty years of ministry on the throne of Peter and as we await the arrival, now imminent, of the third millennium. Despite the limitations brought on by age, I continue to enjoy life. For this I thank the Lord. It is wonderful to be able to give oneself to the very end for the sake of the kingdom of God!

LETTER TO OLDER PEOPLE, October 1, 1999

A disabled person, just like every other weak person, must be encouraged to take charge of his own life. It is therefore the task of the family, having overcome the initial shock, to understand first of all that the value of *life* transcends that of *efficiency*. If it does not understand this, it risks being disappointed and discouraged when, despite every attempt, the hoped-for cure or recovery is not obtained.

THE DIGNITY AND RIGHTS OF DISABLED CHILDREN
Address to the Congress The Family and the Integration of Disabled
Children and Adolescents, December 4, 1999

The final riddle for human beings is death. In looking to Christ, man learns that he himself is destined to live. Christ's Eucharist is the pledge of life. The one who eats Christ's flesh and drinks His blood already has eternal life (see Jn 6:54). Finally, in conquering death by His Resurrection, Christ reveals the resurrection of all; He proclaims life and reveals man to himself in his final destiny, which is life.

Ad Limina ADDRESS TO BISHOPS FROM LOS ANGELES AND SAN
FRANCISCO, July 8, 1988

Christ took upon Himself the whole of human suffering and radically transformed it through the Paschal Mystery of His Passion, Death and Resurrection. The triumph of the Cross gives human suffering a new dimension, a redemptive value.

HOMILY AT MASS IN LOS ANGELES COLISEUM, September 15, 1987

[The elderly] are sometimes forsaken. They suffer because of their old age. They also suffer because of the various troubles that advanced age brings with it. But their greatest suffering is when they do not find the due understanding and gratitude on the part of those from whom they are entitled to expect it.

THE FAMILY: CENTER OF LOVE AND LIFE
General Audience, December 31, 1978

All of us, in some way, experience sorrow and suffering in our lives. No amount of economic, scientific or social progress can eradicate our vulnerability to sin and to death.

HOMILY AT MASS IN LOS ANGELES COLISEUM, September 15, 1987

Suffering, in fact, is always a trial—at times a very hard one—to which humanity is subjected.

APOSTOLIC LETTER ON THE CHRISTIAN MEANING OF HOLY
SUFFERING, 1984

The so-called quality of life is interpreted primarily or exclusively as economic efficiency, inordinate consumerism, physical beauty and pleasure, to the neglect of the more profound dimensions— interpersonal, spiritual and religious—of existence. In such a context suffering, an inescapable burden of human existence but also a factor of possible personal growth, is "censored," rejected as useless, indeed opposed as an evil always and in every way to be avoided. When it cannot be avoided and the prospect of even some future well-being vanishes, then life appears to have lost all meaning and the temptation grows in man to claim the right to suppress it.

ENCYCLICAL: THE GOSPEL OF LIFE (*Evangelium Vitae*), 1994

It can be said that man suffers whenever he experiences any kind of evil. In the Old Testament, suffering and evil are identified with each other.

APOSTOLIC LETTER ON THE CHRISTIAN MEANING

OF HOLY SUFFERING, 1984

In old age, how should one face the inevitable decline of life? How should one act in the face of death? The believer knows that his life is in the hands of God: "You, O Lord, hold my lot" (cf. Ps 16:5), and he accepts from God the need to die: "This is the decree from the Lord for all flesh, and how can you reject the good pleasure of the Most High?" (cf. Sir 41:3–4). Man is not the master of life, nor is he the master of death. In life and in death, he has to entrust himself completely to the "good pleasure of the Most High," to His loving plan.

ENCYCLICAL: THE GOSPEL OF LIFE (*Evangelium Vitae*), 1994

God is on the side of the oppressed. He is beside the parents who cry for their murdered children; He hears the impotent cry of the defenseless and downtrodden; He is in solidarity with women humiliatingly violated; He is near to refugees forced to leave their land and their homes. Do not forget the sufferings of families, of the elderly, widows, the young and children. It is His people who are dying.

HOMILY AT THE MASS FOR SARAJEVO AT CASTEL GANDOLFO,

September 8, 1994

Dear friends! in what happened to the child of Bethlehem you can recognize what happens to children throughout the world. It is true that a child represents the joy not only of its parents but also the joy of the Church and the whole of society. But it is also true that in our days, unfortunately, many children in different parts of the world are suffering and being threatened: They are hungry and poor, they are dying from diseases and malnutrition, they are the victims of war, they are abandoned by their parents and condemned to remain without a home, without the warmth of a family of their own, they suffer many forms of violence and arrogance from grownups. How can we not care, when we see the suffering of so many children, especially when this suffering is in some way caused by grownups?

CHRISTMAS LETTER TO THE WORLD'S CHILDREN,
December 15, 1994

When we have striven to alleviate or overcome suffering, when like Christ we have prayed that "the cup pass us by" (cf. Mt 26:39), and yet suffering remains, then we must walk "the royal road" of the Cross. As I mentioned before, Christ's answer to our question "why?" is above all a call, a vocation. Christ does not give us an abstract answer, but rather He says, "Follow me!" He offers us the opportunity through suffering to take part in His own work of saving the world. And when we do take up our cross, then gradually the salvific meaning of suffering is revealed to us. It is then that in our sufferings we find inner peace and even spiritual joy (cf. *Salvifici Doloris*, 26).

HOMILY AT MASS IN LOS ANGELES COLISEUM, September 15, 1987

Death is not only a "natural" necessity. Death is a mystery. Here we enter the particular time in which the whole Church, more than ever, wishes to meditate on death as the mystery of man in Christ. Christ the Son of God accepted death as a natural necessity, as an inevitable part of man's fate on earth. Jesus Christ accepted death as the consequence of sin. Right from the beginning death was united with sin: the death of the body ("to dust you shall return" [Gn 3:19]) and the death of the human spirit owing to disobedience to God, to the Holy Spirit. Jesus Christ accepted death as a sign of obedience to God, in order to restore to the human spirit the full gift of the Holy Spirit. Jesus Christ accepted death to overcome sin. Jesus Christ accepted death to overcome death in the very essence of its perennial mystery.

ASH WEDNESDAY ADDRESS, March 1979

Pain and sorrow are not endured alone or in vain. Although it remains difficult to understand suffering, Jesus has made it clear that its value is linked to His own suffering and death, to His own sacrifice. In other words, by your suffering you help Jesus in His work of salvation. Your call to suffering requires strong faith and patience. Yes, it means that you are called to love with a special intensity. But remember that our Blessed Mother Mary is close to you, just as she was close to Jesus at the foot of the Cross. And she will never leave you all alone.

ADDRESS AT DUBLIN, September 29, 1979

Earthly suffering, when accepted in love, is like a bitter kernel containing the seed of new life, the treasure of divine glory to be given man in eternity.

VATICAN ADDRESS, April 27, 1994

Especially those who are oppressed by apparently senseless moral suffering find in Jesus' moral suffering the meaning of their own trials and they go with Him into Gethsemani. In Him they find the strength to accept pain with holy abandon and trusting obedience to the Father's will. And they feel rising from within their hearts the prayer of Gethsemani: "But let it be as you would have it, Father, not as I" (Mk 14:36). They mystically identify with Jesus' resolve when He was arrested: "Am I not to drink the cup the Father has given me?" (Jn 18:11). In Christ they also find the courage to offer their pain for the salvation of all, having learned the mysterious fruitfulness of every sacrifice from the offering on Calvary, according to the principle set forth by Jesus: "I solemnly assure you, unless the grain of wheat falls to the earth and dies, it remains just a grain of wheat. But if it dies, it produces much fruit" (Jn 12:24).

VATICAN ADDRESS, April 27, 1994

Man who, according to the laws of nature, is "condemned to death," man who lives in the perspective of the annihilation of his body, exists at the same time in the perspective of future life, and is called to joy.

The solemnity of All Saints puts before the eyes of our faith all those who have already reached the fullness of their call to union with God. The day that commemorates the dead directs our thoughts towards those who, having left this world, are waiting in expiation to reach that fullness of love which union with God requires.

VATICAN ADDRESS, November 1, 1978

The Pope wishes to give special attention to the sick, to bring them an affectionate greeting and a word of comfort and encouragement. You, dear sick people, have an important place in the Church, if you can interpret your difficult situation in the light of faith and if, in this light, you are able to live your illness with a generous and strong heart. Each of you can then affirm with St. Paul: "In my flesh I complete what is lacking in Christ's afflictions for the sake of his body, that is, the church" (Col 1:24).

VATICAN ADDRESS, November 19, 1978

We die in the physical body when all the energies of life are extinguished. We die through sin when love dies in us. Outside of love there is no life. If man opposes love and lives without love, death takes root in his soul and grows. For this reason Christ cries out: "I give you a new commandment: Love one another. Such as my love has been for you, so must your love be for each other" (Jn 13:34). The cry for love is the cry for life, for the victory of the soul over sin and death. The source of this victory is the Cross of Jesus Christ: His Death and His Resurrection.

HOMILY AT MASS AT SAN ANTONIO, September 13, 1987

Brothers in Christ, who know the bitter harshness of the way of the Cross, do not feel that you are alone. The Church is with you as a sacrament of salvation to sustain you in your difficult path. She receives much when you live your suffering with faith; she is beside you with the comfort of active solidarity in her members so that you never lose hope. Remember how Jesus invites you: "Come to me all of you who are weary and tired, and I will give you complete rest" (Mt 11:28).

ADDRESS AT THE VATICAN AIDS CONFERENCE, November 30, 1989

The Church is universal because it has something to offer all peoples and welcomes all countries and cultures into its institutions. The revelation of God in Jesus Christ is subject to no boundaries. Christ is salvation for all humanity.

In another sense, the Catholic Church is universal for what it embodies. Its highest governing body includes representatives from nearly all nations and races. Its churches span the world, from small villages in the remotest parts of Africa to the largest cities in the Western world. Because its truths are universal, its mission is universal as well. The Church's history has touched and will continue to touch the histories of countries and cultures throughout the world.

These are some of the reasons why churches can never be considered individually—each forms a part of a universal physical and spiritual entity. For Pope John Paul II, any church severed from its roots in the universal Church is incomplete. As members of one body, all individual churches contribute to the growth of the universal Church by developing their particular gifts. In return, the universal Church enriches individual churches through its collective experience.

THE UNIVERSAL CHURCH

The specific contribution of the Church—of her members and of her individual communities—to the cause of a new humanism, of true human culture, is the full truth of Christ about humanity: the meaning of humanity, its origin, its destiny and, therefore, its incomparable dignity.

EASTER MESSAGE TO THE BISHOPS OF THE UNITED STATES,
April 3, 1983

The civil authorities of the People's Republic of China should rest assured: a disciple of Christ can live his faith in any political system, provided that there is respect for his right to act according to the dictates of his own conscience and his own faith. For this reason I repeat to the governing authorities, as I have said so often to others, that they should have no fear of God or of His Church. Indeed, I respectfully ask them, in deference to the authentic freedom which is the innate right of every man and woman, to ensure that those also who believe in Christ may increasingly contribute their energies and talents to the development of their country. The Chinese nation has an important role to play in the international community. Catholics can make a notable contribution to this, and they will do so with enthusiasm and commitment.

MESSAGE TO THE CHURCH IN CHINA, December 3, 1996

Jesus Christ taught that man not only receives and experiences the mercy of God, but that he is also called "to practice mercy" towards others: "Blessed are the merciful, for they shall obtain mercy" (Ma 5:7). The Church sees in these words a call to action, and she tries to practice mercy. All the beatitudes of the Sermon on the Mount indicate the way of conversion and of reform of life, but the one referring to those who are merciful is particularly eloquent in this regard. Man attains to the merciful love of God, His mercy, to the extent that he himself is interiorly transformed in the spirit of that love towards his neighbor.

ENCYCLICAL: MERCY OF GOD (Dives in Misericordia), 1980

Following Christ, the Church seeks the truth, which is not always the same as the majority opinion. She listens to conscience and not to power, and in this way she defends the poor and the downtrodden.

APOSTOLIC EXHORTATION Familiaris Consortio, 1981

While remaining faithful to her doctrine and discipline, the Church esteems and honors all cultures; she respects them in all her evangelizing efforts among the various peoples. At the first Pentecost, those present heard the Apostles speaking in their own languages (see Acts 2:4ff). With the guidance of the Holy Spirit, we try in every age to bring the Gospel convincingly and understandably to people of all races, languages and cultures. It is important to realize that there is no black Church, no white Church, no American Church; but there is and must be, in the one Church of Jesus Christ, a home for blacks, whites, Americans, every culture and race.

ADDRESS AT MEETING WITH BLACK CATHOLIC LEADERSHIP,
NEW ORLEANS, September 12, 1987

The Church lives an authentic life when she professes and proclaims mercy—the most stupendous attribute of the Creator and of the Redeemer—and when she brings people close to the sources of the Savior's mercy, of which she is the trustee and dispenser.

ENCYCLICAL: MERCY OF GOD (*Dives in Misericordia*), 1980

The Catholic Church is not confined to a particular territory and she has no geographical borders; her members are men and women of all regions of the world. She knows, from many centuries of experience, that suppression, violation or restriction of religious freedom have caused suffering, bitterness, moral and material hardship, and that even today there are millions of people enduring these evils. By contrast, the recognition, guarantee and respect of religious freedom bring serenity to individuals and peace to the social community; they also represent an important factor in strengthening a nation's moral cohesion, in improving people's common welfare and in enriching the cooperation among nations in an atmosphere of mutual trust.

THE FREEDOM OF CONSCIENCE AND RELIGIONS,
September 1, 1980

Resist the temptation of whatever can weaken communion in the Church as a sacrament of unity and salvation—whether it be from those who make an ideology of the faith or claim to build a "popular Church" which is not that of Christ, or whether it be from those who promote the spread of religious sects which have little to do with the true contents of the faith.

MESSAGE AT SANTO DOMINGO, DOMINICAN REPUBLIC,
October 12, 1984

Now this is the only motive that the Church—and with her the Pope at this moment—has before her eyes and in her heart: that every man may meet Christ in order that Christ may walk with every man along the ways of life.

ADDRESS AT RIO DE JANEIRO, July 10, 1980

The present time is an important moment in the history of the universal Church and, in particular, of the Church in Ireland. So many things have changed. So many valuable new insights have been gained in what it means to be Christian. So many new problems have to be faced by the faithful, either because of the increased pace of change in society or because of the new demands that are made on the People of God—demands to live to the fullest the mission of evangelization.

HOMILY AT THE SHRINE OF OUR LADY OF KNOCK,
MAYO COUNTY, IRELAND, January 1, 1979

Universal by nature, she [the Catholic Church] is conscious of being at the service of all and never identifies with any one national community. She welcomes to her bosom all nations, races and cultures. She is mindful of—indeed she knows that she is the depository of—God's design for humanity: to gather all people into one family. And this because God is the Creator and Father of all. That is the reason why every time that Christianity—whether according to its Western or Eastern tradition—becomes the instrument of a form of nationalism, it is, as it were, wounded in its very heart and made sterile.

THE RISKS ATTACHED TO NATIONALISM
Address to Diplomats, January 15, 1994

The Church sheds light upon temporal realities; she purifies, uplifts and reconciles them to God. This she does, on the one hand, through the presence and action of her members in the world of human affairs and human endeavors. Countless works and institutions, large and small, in every corner of the world testify to the ecclesial community's unfailing commitment and generosity in serving the good of the human family and in meeting the needs of millions of our brothers and sisters. This boundless witness of faith and love on the part of single members of the Church as well as of groups and communities reveals the true face of the Church to the world (cf. *Gaudium et Spes*, 43). It is the fulfillment of Jesus' pressing invitation: "Let your light so shine before men, that they may see your good works and give glory to your Father who is in heaven" (Mt 5:16).

Ad Limina ADDRESS: REFLECTIONS ON THE NEW ENCYCLICAL,
October 15, 1993

The approaching end of the second millennium demands of everyone an examination of conscience and the promotion of fitting ecumenical initiatives so that we can celebrate the Great Jubilee, if not completely united, at least much closer to overcoming the divisions of the second millennium.

Tertio Millennio Adveniente:
APOSTOLIC LETTER FOR THE JUBILEE 2000

How many testimonies of faith, how many messages of fidelity I have received from communities throughout China! Bishops, priests, religious and lay people have wished to reaffirm their unshakable and full communion with Peter and the rest of the Church. As pastor of the universal Church, my heart greatly rejoices at this. I earnestly invite you all to seek paths to communion and reconciliation, paths which draw their light and inspiration from the truth Himself: Jesus Christ.

MESSAGE BROADCAST TO CATHOLICS IN CHINA, January 14, 1995

The Second Vatican Council refers to the Church as a mystery—a mystery of communion. This means that the Church is more than just a community or tradition with shared beliefs and practices, more than an organization with moral influence. Using the imagery of Scripture, the Council also speaks of the Church as a sheepfold, a cultivated field and a building. The Church is Christ's Body, His Bride, and our Mother (cf. *Lumen Gentium*, 6–7). We believe that our communion with Christ and with one another comes into being through the outpouring of the Holy Spirit. We believe too that the Holy Spirit makes it fruitful.

ADDRESS AT DETROIT, September 18, 1987

The universal dimension and the particular dimension constitute two essential sources in the life of the Church: communion and diversity, tradition and new times, the ancient Christian lands and new people coming to the faith. The Church has succeeded in being one and at the same time differentiated. Accepting unity as the first principle, she has taken on different forms in the individual parts of the world. This is true in a particular way for the Western Church and for the Eastern Church before their progressive estrangement from each other.

APOSTOLIC LETTER: GO INTO ALL THE WORLD
(*Euntes in Mundum*), January 25, 1988

The "new evangelization," which the modern world urgently needs and which I have emphasized many times, must include among its essential elements a proclamation of the Church's social doctrine. As in the days of Pope Leo XIII, this doctrine is still suitable for indicating the right way to respond to the great challenges of today, when ideologies are being increasingly discredited. Now, as then, we need to repeat that there can be no genuine solution of the "social question" apart from the Gospel, and that the "new things" can find in the Gospel the context for their correct understanding and the proper moral perspective for judgment on them.

ENCYCLICAL: THE ONE HUNDREDTH YEAR
(*Centesimus Annus*), 1991

The most valuable gift that the Church can offer to the bewildered and restless world of our time is to form within it Christians who are confirmed in what is essential and who are humbly joyful in their faith. Catechesis will teach this to them, and it will itself be the first to benefit from it: "The man who wishes to understand himself thoroughly—and not just in accordance with immediate, partial, often superficial, and even illusory standards and measures of his being—must come to Christ with his unrest and uncertainty, and even his weakness and sinfulness, his life and death. He must, so to speak, enter into Christ with all his own self, he must 'appropriate' Christ and assimilate the whole of the reality of the Incarnation and redemption in order to find himself."

APOSTOLIC EXHORTATION *Christifideles Laici,* December 30, 1988

Finally, dear friends, I think of your insertion into the universal Church. It is a beautiful and great mystery. The tree of the Church, planted by Jesus in the Holy Land, has not stopped developing. All the countries of the old Roman Empire were grafted onto it. My own Polish homeland experienced its hour of evangelization and the Church of Poland has been grafted onto the tree of the Church in order to make it produce new fruits. And now your community of Congolese believers has in its turn been grafted onto the tree of the Church.

HOMILY IN THE CONGO, May 5, 1980

When the Church proclaims God's salvation to man, when she offers and communicates the life of God through the sacraments, when she gives direction to human life through the commandments of love of God and neighbor, she contributes to the enrichment of human dignity. But just as the Church can never abandon her religious and transcendent mission on behalf of man, so too she is aware that today her activity meets with particular difficulties and obstacles. That is why she devotes herself with ever new energies and methods to an evangelization which promotes the whole human being. Even on the eve of the third millennium she continues to be "a sign and safeguard of the transcendence of the human person" as indeed she always sought to be.

ENCYCLICAL: THE ONE HUNDREDTH YEAR
(*Centesimus Annus*), 1991

John Paul believes that women have a dignity and responsibility that is in every way equal to that of men, and that closing any public role to them is contrary to the proper position of women in the world. At the same time, he insists that clear recognition be given to the value of the role of women as wives and mothers. This belief in no way contradicts his conviction that women and men are equal in the workplace. Neither men nor women can ignore the family in favor of work. John Paul also believes that society must be restructured so that women do not have to choose between work and family—that is, he feels that women's rightful place in the world of work should not have to be purchased at the cost of family.

The differences that the Holy Father acknowledges between men and women do not imply the acceptance of male domination. In fact, any domination of one person by another is not a natural state at all but a product of original sin. Discrimination against women, like other types of discrimination, has its roots in the inability to understand and acknowledge that every human being is a child of God.

However firm his belief in the equality of the sexes, the Pope remains a traditionalist. He believes that the choice to remain a virgin or to become a mother is equally worthy, that women cannot be ordained in the priesthood, and that Mary is the model mother and the model woman.

WOMEN

It must be clear that the Church stands firmly against every form of discrimination which in any way compromises the equal dignity of women and men. The complete equality of persons is, however, accompanied by a marvelous complementarity. This complementarity concerns not only the roles of men and women but also, and more deeply, their makeup and meaning as persons.

WOMEN'S ROLES DISCUSSED WITH MEMBERS OF MOTHER MARY MACKILLOP'S ORDER IN AUSTRALIA, January 19, 1995

In dealing with the specific rights of women as women, it is necessary to return again and again to the immutable basis of Christian anthropology as it is foreshadowed in the Scriptural account of the creation of man—as male and female—in the image and likeness of God. Both man and woman are created in the image of the personhood of God, with inalienable personal dignity, and in complementarity one with the other. Whatever violates the complementarity of women and men, whatever impedes the true communion of persons according to the complementarity of the sexes offends the dignity of both women and men.

ADDRESS TO U.S. BISHOPS, September 2, 1988

Toil is something that is universally known, for it is universally experienced. . . . It is familiar to women who, sometimes without proper recognition on the part of society, and even of their own families, bear the daily burden and responsibility for their homes and the upbringing of their children.

ENCYCLICAL: ON HUMAN WORK (*Laborem Exercens*), 1981

As I have stated, and as Archbishop Weakland has pointed out, women are not called to the priesthood. Although the teaching of the Church on this point is quite clear, it in no way alters the fact that women are indeed an essential part of the Gospel plan to spread the Good News of the Kingdom. And the Church is irrevocably committed to this truth.

SPEECH TO BISHOPS AT LOS ANGELES, September 1987

I am convinced that a mistaken anthropology is at the root of the failure of society to understand the Church teaching on the true role of women. That role is in no way diminished but is in fact enhanced by being related in a special way to motherhood—the source of new life—both physical and spiritual.

WOMEN'S ROLES DISCUSSED WITH MEMBERS OF MOTHER MARY
MACKILLOP'S ORDER IN AUSTRALIA, January 19, 1995

Sadly, though, we often see not the exaltation but the exploitation of women in the media. How often are they treated not as persons with an inviolable dignity but as objects whose purpose is to satisfy others' appetite for pleasure or for power? How often is the role of woman as wife and mother undervalued or even ridiculed? How often is the role of women in business or professional life depicted as a masculine caricature, a denial of the specific gifts of feminine insight, compassion and understanding, which so greatly contribute to the civilization of love?

MESSAGE FOR THE THIRTIETH WORLD COMMUNICATIONS DAY,
January 24, 1996

Women themselves can do much to foster better treatment of women in the media: by promoting sound media education programs, by teaching others, especially their families, to be discriminating consumers in the media market, by making known their views to production companies, publishers, broadcasting networks and advertisers with regard to programs and publications which insult the dignity of women or debase their role in society. Moreover, women can and should prepare themselves for positions of responsibility and creativity in the media, not in conflict with or imitation of masculine roles but by impressing their own genius on their work and professional activity.

MESSAGE FOR THE THIRTIETH WORLD COMMUNICATIONS DAY,
January 24, 1996

It is disheartening to know that in today's world, the simple fact of being a female, rather than a male, can reduce the likelihood of being born or surviving childhood. It can mean receiving less adequate nutrition and health care, and it can increase the chance of remaining illiterate and having only limited access, or none at all, even to primary education. . . . I appeal to all men in the Church to undergo, where necessary, a change of heart and to implement, as a demand of their faith, a positive vision of women.

ADDRESS TO A DELEGATION TO THE FOURTH WORLD
CONFERENCE ON WOMEN, August 29, 1995

Women are radically exploited and reduced to a few of their purely biological functions (providing ova and womb) and research looks to the possibility of constructing artificial wombs, the last step to fabricating human beings in the laboratory.

HUMAN CLONING IS IMMORAL
Reflections from the Pontifical Academy for Life, July 9, 1997

It is a sad reflection on the human condition that still today, at the end of the twentieth century, it is necessary to affirm that every woman is equal in dignity to man and a full member of the human family within which she has a distinctive place and vocation that is complementary to but in no way less valuable than man's. In much of the world much still has to be done to meet the educational and health needs of girls and young women so that they may achieve their full potential in society.

CAIRO POPULATION CONFERENCE DRAFT DOCUMENT
CRITICIZED, March 3, 1994

Jesus always showed the greatest esteem and the greatest respect for woman, for every woman, and in particular he was sensitive to female suffering. Going beyond the religious and social barriers of the time, Jesus reestablished woman in her full dignity as a human person before God and before men.

THOUGHTS ON WOMEN
Address to Italian Maids, April 29, 1979

When women are able fully to share their gifts with the whole community, the very way in which society understands and organizes itself is improved and comes to reflect in a better way the substantial unity of the human family. Here we see the most important condition for the consolidation of authentic peace. The growing presence of women in social, economic and political life at the local, national and international levels is thus a very positive development.

WOMEN: TEACHERS OF PEACE, January 1, 1995

In order to be a teacher of peace, a woman must first of all nurture peace within herself. Inner peace comes from knowing that one is loved by God and from the desire to respond to His love. History is filled with marvelous examples of women who, sustained by this knowledge, have been able successfully to deal with difficult situations of exploitation, discrimination, violence and war.

WOMEN: TEACHERS OF PEACE, January 1, 1995

Many women, especially as a result of social and cultural conditioning, do not become fully aware of their dignity. Others are victims of a materialistic and hedonistic outlook which views them as mere objects of pleasure and does not hesitate to organize the exploitation of women, even of young girls, into a despicable trade. Special concern needs to be shown for these women, particularly by other women who, thanks to their own upbringing and sensitivity, are able to help them discover their own inner worth and resources. Women need to help women and to find support in the valuable and effective contributions which associations, movements and groups, many of them of a religious character, have proved capable of making in this regard.

WOMEN: TEACHERS OF PEACE, January 1, 1995

Society should not allow woman's maternal role to be demeaned or count as of little value in comparison with other possibilities. Greater consideration should be given to the social role of mothers, and support should be given to programs which aim at decreasing maternal mortality, providing prenatal and perinatal care, meeting the nutritional needs of pregnant women and nursing mothers, and helping mothers themselves to provide preventive health care for their infants. In this regard, attention should be given to the positive benefits of breast-feeding for nourishment and disease prevention in infants as well as for maternal bonding and birth spacing.

CAIRO POPULATION CONFERENCE DRAFT DOCUMENT
CRITICIZED, March 3, 1994

The legitimate desire to contribute with her own abilities to the common good and the social and economic context itself often brings woman to undertake a professional activity. However, it is necessary to avoid the risk that the family and humanity suffer a loss which impoverishes them, since woman can never be replaced in begetting and rearing children. The authorities should therefore provide for the professional promotion of woman and at the same time safeguard her vocation as a mother and educator with appropriate legislation.

VATICAN ADDRESS, April 24, 1994

Motherhood is woman's vocation. It is an eternal vocation, and it is also a contemporary vocation. "The Mother who understands everything and embraces each of us with her heart": these are the words of a song, sung by young people in Poland, which come into my mind at this moment. The song goes on to announce that today the world is particularly "hungry and thirsty" for that motherhood, which is woman's vocation "physically" and "spiritually," as it is Mary's.

Everything must be done in order that the dignity of this splendid vocation may not be broken in the inner life of the new generations; in order that the authority of the woman-mother may not be diminished in the family, social and public life, and in the whole of our civilization; in all our contemporary legislations, in the organization of work, in publications, in the culture of everyday life, in education and in study: in every field of life.

VATICAN ADDRESS, October 1, 1979

Nevertheless, for woman this task of handing on the faith is not meant to be carried out only in the family, but—as we read in *Christifideles Laici:* "also in the various educational environments and, in broader terms, in all that concerns embracing the word of God, its understanding and its communication, as well as its study, research and theological teaching." These are all indications of the role women have in the field of catechesis, which today has spread into broad and diverse areas, some of which were unthinkable in times past.

VATICAN ADDRESS, July 13, 1994

The presence and the role of women in the life and mission of the Church, although not linked to the ministerial priesthood, remain absolutely necessary and irreplaceable. As the declaration *Inter Insigniores* points out, "The Church desires that Christian women should become fully aware of the greatness of their mission: today their role is of capital importance both for the renewal and humanization of society and for the rediscovery by believers of the true face of the Church."

APOSTOLIC LETTER *Ordinatio Sacerdotalis,* May 26, 1994

While it must be recognized that women have the same right as I to perform various public functions, society must be structured in such a way that wives and mothers are not in practice compelled to work outside the home, and that their families can live and prosper in a dignified way even when they themselves devote their full time to their own family.

Furthermore, the mentality which honors women more for their work outside the home than for their work within the family must be overcome. This requires that men should truly esteem and love women with total respect for their personal dignity, and that society should create and develop conditions favoring work in the home.

APOSTOLIC EXHORTATION *Familiaris Consortio,* 1981

"Work is made for man; not man for work." This is the principle that guides Pope John Paul's thinking about the place of labor in human life. Human work is the unique way that men and women collaborate with God and participate in God's transforming work. Human beings alone share this special role as cocreators with God of this redeemed but unfinished world. Yet the development of the world by human activity is less important than the self-fulfillment to be derived from it. We work together in a community guided by God's word and animated by God's love. Thus work becomes a divine activity, a unifying, sacred, and transforming force.

There is a danger, however, that work may be perverted. Forced work has no dignity, and imposing work on others against their will is ungodly; useless work can be used as punishment; people can be made into machines and worked to exhaustion, or otherwise have their human worth denied by the work they do. In order for work to be sacred, it must be undertaken with free will and in full understanding of its meaning. John Paul urges us to make no distinctions that declare one kind of work more dignified and worthy than another. In this the Lord Himself set the example: "The greatest among you shall serve the rest."

That all work is sacred has practical consequences for John Paul. The Holy Father insists that workers be sufficiently recompensed so that they can provide for themselves and their families, and he encourages minimum wages, health care benefits, pensions, and sick pay as essential parts of the remuneration for any proper work honestly undertaken and worthy of human labor.

WORK

For man and woman thus created and commissioned by God, the ordinary working day has great and wonderful significance. People's ideas, activities and undertakings—however commonplace they may be—are used by the Creator to renew the world, to lead it to salvation, to make it a more perfect instrument of divine glory.

ENCYCLICAL: ON HUMAN WORK (*Laborem Exercens*), 1981

In view of this situation, we must first of all recall a principle that has always been taught by the Church: the principle of the priority of labor over capital.

ENCYCLICAL: ON HUMAN WORK (*Laborem Exercens*), 1981

To you, immigrants who find yourselves unwelcome in the lands where you have moved, we send words of encouragement. The Church has walked alongside generations of migrants in the march for a better life, and she will not cease to stand by you with every kind of service. To seasonal worker who toil stooped under the sun to provide for their families, we unite ourselves in solidarity with you in your quest for just working conditions.

ENCOUNTER WITH JESUS: CONVERSIONS, COMMUNION AND
SOLIDARITY
Message of the Special Assembly for America of the Synod of Bishops,
December 9, 1997

Public authorities therefore have the duty of acting to ensure that these rights are respected and fulfilled, following three basic lines of action:

a. Promotion of conditions that ensure the right to work
b. Guarantee of the right to just remuneration for work
c. Protection and promotion of workers' rights to form associations in order to safeguard their rights; the right of association is a necessary condition for achieving a balance in bargaining power between workers and employers, and hence for guaran-

teeing the development of a correct dialectic between the social parties.

TOWARDS A BETTER DISTRIBUTION OF LAND
Document of the Pontifical Council for Justice and Peace on the
Challenge of Agrarian Reform, November 23, 1997

The Church reminds all who attempt to assert the predominance of technology, thereby reducing man to a "product" or a means of production, that "man is the subject of work," since in the divine plan "work is 'for man' and not man 'for work.'" For the same reason, she also opposes the claims of capitalism, proclaiming "the principle of the priority of labor over capital," since human labor "is always a primary efficient cause, whole capital, the whole collection of means of production, remains a mere instrument or instrumental cause" of the process of production.

CATECHESIS ON THE DIGNITY OF HUMAN WORK, March 19, 1997

An important place in the Church's social doctrine belongs to the right to dignified labor. Consequently, given the high rates of unemployment found in numerous countries in America and the harsh conditions in which many industrial and rural workers find themselves, it is necessary to value work as a factor of the fulfillment and dignity of the human person. It is the ethical responsibility of an organized society to promote and support a culture of work.

ECCLESIA IN AMERICA
Post-synodal Apostolic Exhortation, January 22, 1999

Both the original industrialization that gave rise to what is called the worker question and the subsequent industrial and postindustrial changes show in an eloquent manner that, even in the age of ever more mechanized "work," the proper subject of work continues to be man.

ENCYCLICAL: ON HUMAN WORK (*Laborem Exercens*), 1981

The danger of treating work as a special kind of merchandise, or as an impersonal "force" needed for production (the expression "work force" is, in fact, in common use) always exists, especially when the whole way of looking at the question of economics is marked by the premises of materialistic economism.

ENCYCLICAL: ON HUMAN WORK (*Laborem Exercens*), 1981

Work constitutes a foundation for the formation of family life, which is a natural right and something that man is called to. These two spheres of values . . . must be properly united and must properly permeate each other.

ENCYCLICAL: ON HUMAN WORK (*Laborem Exercens*), 1981

The Church considers it her duty to speak out on work from the viewpoint of its human value and of the moral order to which it belongs, and she sees this as one of her important tasks within the service that she renders to the evangelical message as a whole.

At the same time she sees it as her particular duty to form a spirituality of work which will help all people to come closer, through work, to God, the creator and redeemer, to participate in His salvific plan for man and the world, and to deepen their friendship with Christ in their lives by accepting, through faith, a living participation in His threefold mission as priest, prophet and king, as the Second Vatican Council so eloquently teaches.

ENCYCLICAL: ON HUMAN WORK (*Laborem Exercens*), 1981

God's revelation is profoundly marked by the fundamental truth that man, created in the image of God, shares by his work in the activity of the Creator and that, within the limits of his own human capabilities, man in a sense continues to develop that activity, and perfects it as he advances further and further in the discovery of the resources and values contained in the whole of creation. We find this truth at the very beginning of Sacred Scripture, in the Book of Genesis, where the creation activity itself is presented in the form of "work" done by God during "six days," "resting" on the seventh day.

ENCYCLICAL: ON HUMAN WORK (*Laborem Exercens*), 1981

The knowledge that by means of work man shares in the work of creation constitutes the most profound motive for undertaking it in various sectors. "The faithful, therefore," we read in the constitution *Lumen Gentium,* "must learn the deepest meaning and the value of all creation, and its orientation to the praise of God. Even by their secular activity they must assist one another to live holier lives."

ENCYCLICAL: ON HUMAN WORK (*Laborem Exercens*), 1981

The value of work does not end with the individual. The full meaning of work can only be understood in relation to the family and society as well. Work supports and gives stability to the family. Within the family, moreover, children first learn the human and positive meaning of work and responsibility. In each community and in the nation as a whole, work has a fundamental social meaning. It can, moreover, either join people in the solidarity of a shared commitment or set them at odds through exaggerated competition, exploitation and social conflict. Work is a key to the whole social question, when that "question" is understood to be concerned with making work more human (see *Laborem Exercens, 3*).

HOMILY AT MASS AT LOS ANGELES, September 17, 1987

It [work] is not only good in the sense that it is useful or something to enjoy; it is also good as being something worthy, that is to say, something that corresponds to man's dignity, that expresses this dignity and increases it. If one wishes to define more clearly the ethical meaning of work, that is the truth that one must particularly keep in mind. Work is a good thing for man—a good thing for his humanity—because through work man not only transforms nature, adapting it to his own needs, but he also achieves fulfillment as a human being and indeed, in a sense, becomes "more a human being."

ENCYCLICAL: ON HUMAN WORK (*Laborem Exercens*), 1981

Work is, as has been said, an obligation, that is to say a duty, on the part of man. This is true in all the many meanings of the word. Man must work, both because the Creator has commanded it and because of his own humanity, which requires work in order to be maintained and developed. Man must work out of regard for others, especially his own family, but also for the society he belongs to, the country of which he is a child and the whole human family of which he is a member, since he is the heir to the work of generations and at the same time a sharer in building the future of those who will come after him in the succession of history. All this constitutes the moral obligation of work, understood in its wide sense.

ENCYCLICAL: ON HUMAN WORK (*Laborem Exercens*), 1981

As we view the whole human family throughout the world, we cannot fail to be struck by a disconcerting fact of immense proportions: the fact that, while conspicuous natural resources remain unused, there are huge numbers of people who are unemployed or underemployed and countless multitudes of people suffering from hunger. This is a fact that without any doubt demonstrates that both within the individual political communities and in their relationships on the continental and world level there is something wrong with the organization of work and employment, precisely at the most critical and socially most important points.

ENCYCLICAL: ON HUMAN WORK (*Laborem Exercens*), 1981

Emigration in search of work must in no way become an opportunity for financial or social exploitation. As regards the work relationship, the same criteria should be applied to immigrant workers as to all other workers in the society concerned. The value of work should be measured by the same standard and not according to the difference in nationality, religion or race. For even greater reason the situation of constraint in which the emigrant may find himself should not be exploited.

ENCYCLICAL: ON HUMAN WORK (*Laborem Exercens*), 1981

The true advancement of women requires that labor should be structured in such a way that women do not have to pay for their advancement by abandoning what is specific to them and at the expense of the family, in which women as mothers have an irreplaceable role.

ENCYCLICAL: ON HUMAN WORK (*Laborem Exercens*), 1981

The Church is convinced that work is a fundamental dimension of man's existence on earth.

ENCYCLICAL: ON HUMAN WORK (*Laborem Exercens*), 1981

This Pope has held out an open hand to all world religions. Making it a point to travel widely and to address diverse religious groups, including Jews, Muslims, Buddhists, Shintoists, and Hindus, in sites all over the world, he has enthusiastically embraced religious diversity and called for an end to religious prejudice, racial antagonism, and xenophobia.

In the spirit of brotherhood, he has opposed proselytizing in favor of a broad acceptance of other faiths, acknowledging that God loves and accepts all believing humankind. He has demonstrated this not only by attending worship in other religious sites but also by calling for a "dialogue of life" between all believers in order to "promote moral values, social justice, liberty and peace." In attempting to reach out and build bridges of dialogue, he gathered leaders of all the world's major religions at Assisi, Italy, for a day of prayer for peace in the world.

John Paul II has occasionally stirred controversy with an inadvertent misinterpretation of other religious traditions, as when he described Buddhism (in December 1994, in Sri Lanka) as in large measure an "atheistic system." The result was that Buddhist monks boycotted a Pan-Asian meeting attended by Muslim and Hindu leaders. Moreover, the Pope's—and the Church's—commitment to the proclamation of the Gospel as "the way, the truth, and the life" sometimes seems in conflict with John Paul's goal to achieve world brotherhood and understanding. Similarly, despite ambitions for ecumenical harmony, he has sometimes been unyielding in his approach to the Church's dialogue with other Christian faiths. Yet, as a philosopher and theologian—committed as he is to the traditional creeds and precepts of Roman Catholicism—he nonetheless remains open to rethinking his own positions, looking for new ideas, and encouraging dialogue and reconciliation with all other faiths and religious positions.

WORLD RELIGIONS

Especially since the Second Vatican Council, the Catholic Church has been fully committed to pursuing the path of dialogue and cooperation with members of other religions. Interreligious dialogue is a precious means by which the followers of the various religions discover shared points of contact in the spiritual life, while acknowledging the differences which exist between them. The Church respects the freedom of individuals to seek the truth and to embrace it according to the dictates of conscience, and in this light she firmly rejects proselytism and the use of unethical means to gain conversions.

ADDRESS AT MEETING IN SRI LANKA BOYCOTTED BY BUDDHIST
LEADERS, January 21, 1995

To the Buddhist Community, which reflects numerous Asian traditions as well as American: I wish respectfully to acknowledge your way of life, based upon compassion and loving kindness and upon a yearning for peace, prosperity and harmony for all beings. May all of us give witness to compassion and loving kindness in promoting the true good of humanity.

To the Islamic Community: I share your belief that mankind owes its existence to the One, Compassionate God who created heaven and earth. In a world in which God is denied or disobeyed, in a world that experiences so much suffering and is so much in need of God's mercy, let us then strive together to be courageous bearers of hope.

To the Hindu Community: I hold in esteem your concern for inner peace and for the peace of the world, based not purely on mechanistic or materialistic political considerations, but on self-purification, unselfishness, love and sympathy for all. May the minds of all people be imbued with such love and understanding.

To the Jewish Community: I repeat the Second Vatican Council's conviction that the Church "cannot forget that she received the revelation of the Old Testament through the people with whom

God in His mercy established the Ancient Covenant. Nor can she forget that she draws sustenance from the root of that good olive tree onto which has been grafted the wild olive branches of the Gentiles" (see Rom 11:17–24; *Nostra Aetate*, 4). With you, I oppose every form of anti-Semitism. May we work for the day when all peoples and nations may enjoy security, harmony and peace.

SPEECH TO INTERRELIGIOUS LEADERS AT LOS ANGELES,
September 16, 1987

Just as countries of Christian tradition welcome Muslim communities, certain countries with a Muslim majority also generously welcome non-Muslim communities, allowing them even to build their own places of worship and to live in those countries in accordance with their beliefs. Others, however, continue to practice discrimination against Jews, Christians and other religious groups, going even so far as to refuse them the right to meet in private for prayer. It cannot be said too often: this is an intolerable and unjustifiable violation not only of all the norms of current international law, but of the most fundamental human freedom, that of practicing one's faith openly, which for human beings is their reason for living.

ADDRESS TO DIPLOMATIC CORPS OF THE HOLY SEE,
January 13, 1996

In the Church no one is a stranger, and the Church is not foreign to anyone, anywhere. As a sacrament of unity and thus a sign and a binding force for the whole human race, the Church is the place where illegal immigrants are also recognized and accepted as brothers and sisters. It is the task of the various dioceses actively to ensure that these people, who are obliged to live outside the safety net of civil society, may find a sense of brotherhood in the Christian community.

MESSAGE FOR WORLD MIGRATION DAY, July 25, 1995

All the motives and expressions of the phenomenon of fundamentalism must be examined. The analysis of political, social and economic situations shows that the phenomenon is not only religious, but that in many cases religion is exploited for political ends or, indeed, to compensate for problems of a social and economic

nature. There can be no really lasting response to the phenomenon of fundamentalism as long as the problems that create or sustain it are left unresolved. Although the intolerance and violence
provoked by fundamentalism must be condemned, it is of the
utmost importance to look with faith and love on those who
adopt these attitudes and who frequently suffer from them.

DIALOGUE WITH MUSLIMS, August 26, 1995

In fact in the Christian world—I do not say on the part of the
Church as such—erroneous and unjust interpretations of the
New Testament regarding the Jewish people and their alleged
culpability have circulated for too long, engendering feelings of
hostility towards this people. They contributed to the lulling of
consciences, so that when the wave of persecutions inspired by a
pagan anti-Semitism, which in essence is equivalent to an anti-
Christianity, swept across Europe, alongside Christians who did
everything even at the risk of their lives, the spiritual resistance of
many was not what humanity rightfully expected from the disciples of Christ.

ROOTS OF ANTI-JUDAISM
Address at a Symposium Sponsored by the Historical-Theological
Commission of the Committee for the Great Jubilee of the Year 2000,
October 31, 1997

In this place of memories, the mind and heart and soul feel an
extreme need for silence. Silence in which to remember. Silence
in which to try to make some sense of the memories that come
flooding back. Silence because there are no words strong enough
to deplore the terrible tragedy of the Shoah. My own personal
memories are of all that happened when the Nazis occupied
Poland during the war. I remember my Jewish friends and neighbors, some of whom perished, while others survived.

THE SHOAH AND CHRISTIAN MEMORY
Address to Holocaust Survivors at Yad Vashem Holocaust Memorial,
March 23, 2000

Here, as at Auschwitz and many other places in Europe, we are
overcome by the echo of the heartrending laments of so many.
Men, women and children cry out to us from the depths of the

horror that they knew. How can we fail to heed their cry? No one can forget or ignore what happened. No one can diminish its scale.

THE SHOAH AND CHRISTIAN MEMORY
Address to Holocaust Survivors at Yad Vashem Holocaust Memorial,
March 23, 2000

We wish to remember. But we wish to remember for a purpose, namely to ensure that never again will evil prevail, as it did for the millions of innocent victims of Nazism. How could man have such utter contempt for man? Because he had reached the point of contempt for God. Only a godless ideology could plan and carry out the extermination of a whole people.

THE SHOAH AND CHRISTIAN MEMORY
Address to Holocaust Survivors at Yad Vashem Holocaust Memorial,
March 23, 2000

As Bishop of Rome and successor of the apostle Peter, I assure the Jewish people that the Catholic Church, motivated by the Gospel law of truth and love and by no political considerations, is deeply saddened by the hatred, acts of persecution and displays of anti-Semitism directed against Jews by Christians at any time and in any place. The Church rejects racism in any form as a denial of the image of the Creator inherent in every human being.

THE SHOAH AND CHRISTIAN MEMORY
Address to Holocaust Survivors at Yad Vashem Holocaust Memorial,
March 23, 2000

Let us build a new future in which there will be no more anti-Jewish feeling among Christians or anti-Christian feeling among Jews, but rather the mutual respect required of those who adore the one Creator and Lord, and look to Abraham as our common father in faith.

THE SHOAH AND CHRISTIAN MEMORY
Address to Holocaust Survivors at Yad Vashem Holocaust Memorial,
March 23, 2000

Thank you for the support that your presence here this evening gives to the hope and conviction of so many people that we are indeed entering a new era of interreligious dialogue. We are conscious that closer ties among all believers are a necessary and urgent condition for securing a more just and peaceful world.

THREE FAITHS IN SEARCH OF UNDERSTANDING AND PEACE
Address at a Meeting with Jewish, Christian, and Muslim Religious
Leaders, Jerusalem, March 23, 2000

For all of us Jerusalem, as its name indicates, is the "City of Peace." Perhaps no other place in the world communicates the sense of transcendence and divine election that we perceive in her stones and monuments, and in the witness of the three religious living side by side within her walls. Not everything has been, or will be, easy in this coexistence. But we must find in our respective religious traditions the wisdom and the superior motivation to ensure the triumph of mutual understanding and cordial respect.

THREE FAITHS IN SEARCH OF UNDERSTANDING AND PEACE
Address at a Meeting with Jewish, Christian, and Muslim Religious
Leaders, Jerusalem, March 23, 2000

Religion is the enemy of exclusion and discrimination, of hatred and rivalry, of violence and conflict. Religion is not, and must not become, an excuse for violence, particularly when religious identity coincides with cultural and ethnic identity. Religion and peace go together! Religious belief and practice cannot be separated from the defense of the image of God in every human being.

THREE FAITHS IN SEARCH OF UNDERSTANDING AND PEACE
Address at a Meeting with Jewish, Christian, and Muslim Religious
Leaders, Jerusalem, March 23, 2000

As for non-Christian religions, the Catholic Church rejects nothing in them which is true and holy. Hence, with regard to other religions Catholics intend to emphasize elements of truth wherever they are to be found, while at the same time firmly bearing witness to the newness of the revelation of Christ, preserved in its fullness by the Church. Consistent with this attitude, they reject as alien to the spirit of Christ any discrimination or persecution directed against persons on the basis of race, color, condition of life or religion. Difference of religion must never be a cause of violence or war. Instead persons of different beliefs must feel themselves drawn, precisely because of these beliefs, to work together for peace and justice.

ECCLESIA IN AMERICA
Post-synodal Apostolic Exhortation, January 22, 1999

If Christians must consider themselves brothers of all men, and behave accordingly, this holy obligation is all the more binding when they find themselves before members of the Jewish people. In the "Declaration on the Relationship of the Church with Judaism," in April of this year, the Bishops of the Federal Republic of Germany put this sentence at the beginning: "Whoever meets Jesus Christ, meets Judaism." I would like to make these words mine, too.

ADDRESS TO THE JEWISH COMMUNITY OF WEST GERMANY,
November 17, 1979

The memory of that triumph [of evil] can only fill us with deep bitterness, in fraternal solidarity with those who bear the indelible mark of those tragedies. Let us pray and work so that this doesn't happen. Never again anti-Semitism. Never again the arrogance of nationalisms. Never again genocides.

SPEECH MARKING THE FIFTIETH ANNIVERSARY OF THE
LIBERATION OF AUSCHWITZ, ROME, January 29, 1995

Where Catholics are concerned, it will continue to be an explicit and very important part of my mission to repeat and emphasize that our attitude to the Jewish religion should be one of the greatest respect, since Catholic faith is rooted in the eternal truths contained in the Hebrew Scriptures, and in the irrevocable covenant made with Abraham. We, too, gratefully hold these same truths of our Jewish heritage and look upon you as our brothers and sisters in the Lord.

ADDRESS TO THE JEWISH COMMUNITY OF SYDNEY, AUSTRALIA,
November 26, 1986

Abraham, our common ancestor, teaches all of us, Christians, Jews and Muslims, to follow this way of mercy and love.

ADDRESS AT LISBON, May 14, 1982

I am sure also that faith in the one God can be a powerful leaven of harmony and collaboration among Christians, Jews and Muslims in the struggle against the prejudices and suspicions that ought to be overcome. In the same spirit of respect and friendship, I do not hesitate to address the inhabitants of this country who are nonbelievers, or who are troubled by doubt regarding the faith. We often have in common a loyal dedication to the same humanitarian causes, the concern for justice, fellowship, peace, respect for human dignity and help to the most disadvantaged. I extend my best wishes to you and to your families.

ADDRESS TO FRENCH CATHOLICS AT LOURDES, August 15, 1983

Towering high over all this world, like an ideal center, a precious jewel-case, that keeps the treasures, is the Holy City, Jerusalem, today the object of a dispute that seems without a solution, tomorrow—if people only want it!—tomorrow a crossroads of reconciliation and peace.

HOMILY AT OTRANTO, October 5, 1980

Considering history in the light of the principles of faith in God, we must also reflect on the catastrophic event of the Shoah, that ruthless and inhuman attempt to exterminate the Jewish people in Europe, an attempt that resulted in millions of victims—including women and children, the elderly and the sick—exterminated only because they were Jews. Considering the mystery of the suffering of Israel's children, their witness of hope, of faith and of humanity under dehumanizing outrages, the Church experiences ever more deeply her common bond with the Jewish people and with their treasure of spiritual riches in the past and in the present.

ADDRESS AT MIAMI, September 10, 1987

Your native cultures are the wealth of the peoples, effective ways for transmitting the faith, representations of your relation with God, with men and with the world. They therefore deserve the greatest respect, esteem, sympathy and support on the part of all mankind. These cultures, in fact, have left remarkable monuments—such as those of the Maya, Aztecs, Incas and many others—which we still contemplate today with wonder.

MESSAGE TO PEASANTS AT QUEZALTENANGO, GUATEMALA,
March 7, 1983

The power of truth leads us to recognize with Mahatma Gandhi the dignity, equality and fraternal solidarity of all human beings, and it prompts us to reject every form of discrimination. It shows us once again the need for mutual understanding, acceptance and collaboration between religious groups in the pluralist society of modern India and throughout the world.

ADDRESS AT RAG GHAT, INDIA, January 10, 1986

The victory of life over death is what every human being desires. All religions, especially the great religious traditions followed by most of the peoples of Asia, bear witness to how deeply the truth regarding our immortality is inscribed in man's religious consciousness. Man's search for life after death finds definitive fulfillment in the resurrection of Christ. Because the risen Christ is the demonstration of God's response to this deeply felt longing of the human spirit, the Church professes: "I believe in the resurrection of the body and in life everlasting" (Apostles' Creed). The risen Christ assures the men and women of every age that they are called to a life beyond the frontier of death.

ADDRESS TO MANILA WORLD YOUTH DAY, January 14, 1995

Shintoism, the traditional religion of Japan, affirms for example that all men are equally sons of God and that, because of this, all men are brothers. Moreover, in your religious tradition, you show a special sensitivity and appreciation for the harmony and beauty of nature, and you show a readiness to recognize there a revelation of God the Most High. I am also aware that in your noble teaching on personal asceticism you seek to make the heart of man ever more pure.

The many things that we hold in common impel us to unite ever more closely in friendship and brotherhood in the service of all humanity.

ADDRESS AT THE VATICAN, February 21, 1979

Jerusalem contains communities of believers full of life, whose presence the peoples of the whole world regard as a sign and source of hope—especially those who consider the Holy City to be in a certain way their spiritual heritage and a symbol of peace and harmony. Indeed insofar as she is the homeland of the hearts of all the spiritual descendants of Abraham who hold her very dear, and the place where, according to faith, the created things of earth encounter the infinite transcendence of God, Jerusalem stands out as a symbol of the coming together, or union, and of universal peace for the human family.

APOSTOLIC LETTER *Redemptionis Anno,* 1984

[The dialogue with people of other religions] is a complex of human activities, all founded upon respect and esteem for people of different religions. It includes the daily living together in peace and mutual help, with each bearing witness to the values learned through the experience of faith. It means a readiness to cooperate with others for the betterment of humanity, and a commitment to search together for true peace. It means the encounter of theologians and other religions, areas of convergence and divergence. Where circumstances permit, it means a sharing of spiritual experiences and insights. This sharing can take the form of coming together as brothers and sisters to pray to God in ways which safeguard the uniqueness of each religious tradition.

ADDRESS TO THE MEMBERS AND STAFF OF THE SECRETARIAT
FOR NON-CHRISTIANS, April 28, 1987

Just as we Catholics invite our Christian brethren to share in our initiatives, so too we declare that we are ready to collaborate in theirs, and we welcome the invitations presented to us. In this pursuit of integral human development we can also do much with the members of other religions, as in fact is being done in various places.

ENCYCLICAL: ON SOCIAL CONCERNS (*Sollicitudo Rei Socialis*), 1987

All Christians must, therefore, be committed to dialogue with the believers of all religions, so that mutual understanding and collaboration may grow; so that moral values may be strengthened; so that God may be praised in all creation. Ways must be developed to make this dialogue become a reality everywhere, but especially in Asia, the continent that is the cradle of ancient cultures and religions. Likewise the Catholics and the Christians of other churches must join together in the search for full unity, in order that Christ may become ever more manifest in the love of His followers.

RADIO BROADCAST TO ASIA FROM JAPAN, February 21, 1981

Many innocent people of different nationalities [died in Nazi concentration camps] but in particular, the children of the Jewish people, for whom the Nazi regime had planned a systematic extermination, suffered the dramatic experience of the Holocaust. . . . The consideration of mitigating circumstances does not exonerate the Church from the obligation to express profound regret for the weaknesses of so many of her sons and daughters who sullied her face.

SPEECH MARKING THE FIFTIETH ANNIVERSARY OF THE LIBERATION OF AUSCHWITZ, ROME, January 29, 1995

Dear brothers and sisters of these religions and every religion: so many people today experience inner emptiness even amid material prosperity, because they overlook the great questions of life: What is man? What is the meaning and purpose of life? What is goodness and what is sin? What gives rise to suffering and what purpose does it serve? What is the path to true happiness? What is death, judgment and retribution after death? What, finally, is that ultimate, ineffable mystery which embraces our existence, from which we take our origin and toward which we move?

These profoundly spiritual questions, which are shared to some degree by all religions, also draw us together in a common concern for man's earthly welfare, especially world peace.

SPEECH TO INTERRELIGIOUS LEADERS AT LOS ANGELES, September 16, 1987

Pope John Paul is devoted to children and young people, and has addressed them often, all over the world. Our fondness and regard for children and the young—as measured by our response to their needs—is a test of our regard for human beings in general. No society that does not highly value the young can long survive, and the Pope himself finds a positive delight in them: "I wish to express," he has said, "the joy that we all find in children, the springtime of life, the anticipation of the future." It must also be said that John Paul finds this joy in all children, including the handicapped and the sick, and he encourages parents and others to lavish attention on children with special needs.

For John Paul, the family is at the center of a child's or a young person's life. The family is the single most important provider of education, and the Christian family is the model for a properly ordered society. Especially in industrialized societies, parents may be tempted to evade the responsibility for education, leaving it to the mass media or other institutions. John Paul sees this as a danger to be avoided at all costs and insists that parents help children develop a sense of judgment about their sources of information and entertainment. It is the family, led by parents, that offers youth their finest and most essential foundation, whether religious, moral, or cultural.

In all the discoveries to be made in youth, the most important to the Holy Father is the discovery of Christ—the personal discovery of the Lord.

YOUTH

Again and again I find in young people the joy and enthusiasm of
life, a searching for truth and for the deeper meaning of the existence that unfolds before them in all its attraction and potential.

SPEECH AT BOSTON COMMON, October 1, 1979

Students who have completed their studies abroad, thanks to
their professional preparation, can offer the necessary drive to lead
their country out of the shallows of underdevelopment. To invest
in their formation should therefore be one of the preferred forms
of cooperation. It is important that these same students should be
aware of their responsibility to their homeland. One of the keys
to its development is in their hands: they must not shrink from
this responsibility! They must not deprive their homeland of the
skills that they have acquired as physicians, engineers, agrono-
mists or experts in one field or another of social life. As Christians, they must feel obliged to make a Gospel option of service
to the poor, thus becoming living stones of the community that
begot them in the faith. They will therefore diligently attend to
their cultural improvement and spiritual formation, in order to
be peacemakers and messengers of a more united, reconciled and
free world.

LETTER TO ARCHBISHOP GIOVANNI, June 16, 1996

To you young people, I say: If you hear the Lord's call, do not
reject it! Dare to become part of the great movements of holiness
which renowned saints have launched in their following of
Christ. Cultivate the ideals proper to your age, but readily accept
God's plan for you if He invites you to seek holiness in the consecrated life. Admire all God's works in the world, but be ready to
fix your eyes on the things destined never to pass away. The third
millennium awaits the contribution of the faith and creativity of
great numbers of young consecrated persons that the world may
be made more peaceful and able to welcome God and, in Him, all
His sons and daughters.

EXHORTATION ON THE CONSECRATED LIFE, March 25, 1996

Children are not only victims of the violence of wars; many are forced to take an active part in them. In some countries of the world it has come to the point where even very young boys and girls are compelled to serve in the armies of the warring parties. Enticed by the promise of food and schooling, they are confined to remote camps where they suffer hunger and abuse and are encouraged to kill even people from their own villages. Often they are sent ahead to clear minefields. Clearly, the life of children has little value for those who use them this way!

MESSAGE FOR WORLD DAY OF PEACE, August 8, 1995

I ask you young people, who naturally and instinctively make your love of life the horizon of your dreams and the rainbow of your hopes, to become prophets of life. Be such by your words and deeds, rebelling against the civilization of selfishness that often considers the human person a means rather than an end, sacrificing its dignity and feelings in the name of mere profit. Do so by concretely helping those who need you and who perhaps, without your help, would be tempted to resign themselves to despair.

ADDRESS FOR WORLD YOUTH DAY, November 26, 1995

We turn with heavy hearts to the bitter hardships borne by you, the children of the streets. What you, the children of God, suffer should happen to no one. Sometimes you may not even realize that you are abandoned, abused, exploited and entangled in a life of crime. Some of you are even living under the threat of murder by those who should shield you from harm. We call on people of good will to help rescue you from these dangers, so you may enjoy a secure and normal life and discover the presence of God's love.

ENCOUNTER WITH JESUS: CONVERSIONS, COMMUNION

AND SOLIDARITY

Message of the Special Assembly for America of the Synod of Bishops, December 9, 1997

We know of the many hardships faced by you, young men and women, who leave your homes in rural areas for the uncertainties and impersonal life of the city and who emigrate from your native lands to begin a new life in a strange land, where you are often misunderstood and mistreated. To all of you, we offer the renewed promise of God's love in the community of the Church and fellowship with us as we labor together to build up the kingdom of God.

ENCOUNTER WITH JESUS: CONVERSIONS, COMMUNION
AND SOLIDARITY
Message of the Special Assembly for America of the Synod of Bishops,
December 9, 1997

Everywhere young people are asking important questions—questions on the meaning of life, on the right way to live, on the true scale of values: "What must I do . . . ?" "What must I do to share in everlasting life?" This questioning bears witness to your thoughts, your consciences, your hearts and wills. This questioning tells the world that you, young people, carry within yourselves a special openness with regard to what is good and what is true.

SPEECH AT BOSTON COMMON, October 1, 1979

Your mission as young people today is to the whole world. In what sense? You can never forget the interdependence of human beings wherever they are. When Jesus tells us to love our neighbor He does not set a geographical limit. What is needed today is a solidarity between all the young people of the world—a solidarity especially with the poor and all those in need. You young people must change society by your lives of justice and fraternal love. It is not just a question of your own country, but of the whole world. This is certainly your mission, dear young people. You are partners with each other, partners with the whole Church, partners with Christ.

ADDRESS AT NEW ORLEANS, September 12, 1987

University students . . . are in a splendid position to take to heart the Gospel invitation to go out of themselves, to reject introversion and to concentrate on the needs of others. Students with the opportunities of higher education can readily grasp the relevance for today of Christ's parable of the rich man and Lazarus (see Lk 16:19ff), with all of its consequences for humanity. What is at stake is not only the rectitude of individual human hearts but also the whole social order as it touches the spheres of economy, politics and human rights and relations.

ADDRESS AT WESTOVER HILLS, TEXAS, September 13, 1987

You will hear people tell you that your religious practices are hopelessly out of date, that they hamper your style and your future, that with everything that social and scientific progress has to offer, you will be able to organize your own lives, and that God has played out His role. Even many religious persons will adopt such attitudes, breathing them in from the surrounding atmosphere without attending to the practical atheism that is at their origin.

REMARKS TO YOUTH IN GALWAY, IRELAND, September 30, 1979

Yes, dear young people, do not close your eyes to the moral sickness that stalks your society today, and from which your youth alone will not protect you. How many young people have already warped their consciences and have substituted the true joy of life with drugs, sex, alcohol, vandalism and the empty pursuit of mere material possessions.

REMARKS TO YOUTH IN GALWAY, IRELAND, September 30, 1979

Each successive World Youth Day has been a confirmation of young people's openness to the meaning of life as a gift received, a gift to which they are eager to respond by striving for a better world for themselves and their fellow human beings. I believe that we should correctly interpret their deepest aspirations by saying that what they ask is that society—especially the leaders of nations and all who control the destinies of peoples—accept them as true partners in the construction of a more humane, more just, more compassionate world. They ask to be able to contribute their specific ideas and energies to this task.

REMARKS AT WELCOMING CEREMONIES AT REGIS COLLEGE,
DENVER, August 12, 1993

In my pastoral visits to the Church in every part of the world, I have been deeply moved by the almost universal conditions of difficulty in which young people grow up and live. Too many sufferings are visited upon them by natural calamities, famines, epidemics, by economic and political crises, by the atrocities of wars.

And where material conditions are at least adequate, other obstacles arise, not the least of which is the breakdown of family values and stability. In developed countries, a serious moral crisis is already affecting the lives of many young people, leaving them adrift, often without hope and conditioned to look only for instant gratification. Yet everywhere there are young men and women deeply concerned about the world around them, ready to give the best of themselves in service to others and particularly sensitive to life's transcendent meaning.

REMARKS AT WELCOMING CEREMONIES AT REGIS COLLEGE,
DENVER, August 12, 1993

We do not ask the young people to abandon their uncertainties, questions or criticisms. Rather we ask all those who call themselves Christians to allow themselves to be guided by grace to encounter Christ in the Church, through the sacraments, prayer and the reception of the Word.

INTERNATIONAL YOUTH FORUM'S MESSAGE TO THE WORLD'S
YOUTH, August 26, 1993

Young people of World Youth Day, the Church asks you to go, in the power of the Holy Spirit, to those who are near and those who are far away. Share with them the freedom you have found in Christ. People thirst for genuine inner freedom. They yearn for the life which Christ came to give in abundance. The world at the approach of a new millennium, for which the whole Church is preparing, is like a field ready for the harvest. Christ needs laborers ready to work in His vineyard. May you, the Catholic young people of the world, not fail Him. In your hands, carry the cross of Christ. On your lips, the words of life. In your hearts, the saving grace of the Lord.

A CELEBRATION OF LIFE
Homily at Cherry Creek State Park, Aurora, Colorado, August 15, 1993

Parents and older people sometimes feel that they have lost contact with you, and they are upset, just as Mary and Joseph felt anguish when they realized that Jesus had stayed behind in Jerusalem. Sometimes you are very critical of the world of adults, and sometimes they are very critical of you. This is not something new, and it is not always without real basis in life. But always remember that you owe your life and upbringing to your parents, and the Fourth Commandment expresses in a concise way the demands of justice toward them (cf. Catechism of the Catholic Church, 2215).

In most cases, they have provided for your education at the cost of personal sacrifice. Thanks to them you have been introduced to the cultural and social heritage of your community and country. Generally speaking, your parents have been your first teachers in the faith. Parents therefore have a right to expect from their sons and daughters the mature fruits of their efforts, just as children and young people have the right to expect from their parents the love and care which lead to a healthy development. I am asking you to build bridges of dialogue and communication with your parents. Be a healthy influence on society to help to break down the barriers which have been raised between generations!

HOMILY AT THE CLOSING MASS OF MANILA WORLD YOUTH DAY,
January 15, 1995

We cannot ignore the deep desires that are stirring in people's hearts today. In spite of negative signs, many hunger for an authentic and challenging spirituality. There is "a fresh discovery of God in His transcendent reality as the infinite Spirit" (*Dominum et Vivificantem,* 2), and young people especially are looking for a solid foundation upon which to build their lives. The youth of America look to you to lead them to Christ, who is the only "existentially adequate response to the desire in every human heart for goodness, truth and life" (*Centesimus Annus,* 24). Allow me to repeat what I said to the bishops last month in Denver: "Are we always ready to help the young people discover the transcendent elements of Christian life? From our words and actions do they conclude that the Church is indeed a mystery of communion with the Blessed Trinity and not just a human institution with temporal aims?" (Homily, August 13, 1993).

ACCOMPANYING YOUTH IN THEIR PILGRIMAGE OF FAITH
Ad Limina Address, September 21, 1993

What do the Church and the Pope expect of the young people of the Tenth World Youth Day? That you confess Jesus Christ. And that you learn to proclaim all that the message of Christ contains for the true liberation and genuine progress of humanity. This is what Christ expects of you. This is what the Church looks for in the young people of the Philippines, of Asia, of the world.

ADDRESS TO MANILA WORLD YOUTH DAY, January 14, 1995

Young people, I say to you, Christ is waiting for you with open arms: Christ is relying on you to build justice and peace, to spread love. As in Turin, I say again today: "You must return to the school of Christ to rediscover the true, full, deep meaning of these words. The necessary support for these values lies only in posses- sion of a sure and sincere faith, a faith that embraces God and man, man in God. . . . There is not a more adequate, a deeper dimension to give to this word 'man,' to this word 'love,' to this word 'freedom,' to this word 'peace' and 'justice': there is nothing else, there is only Christ."

ADDRESS TO THE SACRED COLLEGE OF CARDINALS,
December 22, 1980

Where there are young people, adolescents, children, there is the guarantee of joy, since it is life in its most spontaneous and most exuberant bloom. You possess this *joie de vivre* abundantly and bestow it generously on a world that is sometimes tired, discour- aged, disheartened, disappointed. This meeting of ours is also a sign of hope, because adults, not only your parents, but also your teachers, professors and all those who collaborate in your physical and intellectual growth and development, see in you those who will attain what they, perhaps—owing to various circumstances— have not been able to achieve.

VATICAN ADDRESS, November 22, 1978

There is always a special attraction in you young people, because of that instinctive goodness of yours not contaminated by evil, and because of your particular readiness to accept truth, and put it into practice. And since God is truth, you, loving and accepting truth, are nearest to heaven.

VATICAN ADDRESS, December 13, 1978

Come particularly you, young people, thirsty for innocence, con- templation, interior beauty, pure joy; you who seek the ultimate and decisive meaning of existence and history, come, and recognize and enjoy Christian and Benedictine spirituality, before letting yourselves be attracted by other experiences!

ADDRESS AT MONTE CASSINO ABBEY, May 18, 1979

The Church needs you. The world needs you, because it needs Christ, and you belong to Christ. And so I ask you to accept your responsibility in the Church, the responsibility of your Catholic education: to help—by your words and, above all, by the example of your lives—to spread the Gospel. You do this by praying, and by being just and truthful and pure. Dear young people: by a real Christian life, by the practice of your religion you are called to give witness to your faith. And because actions speak louder than words, you are called to proclaim by the conduct of your daily lives that you really do believe that Jesus Christ is Lord!

ADDRESS AT NEW YORK CITY, October 3, 1979

The selections in this section offer a sampling of the wisdom of the Pope on vital themes and aspects of Christian life. These selections cover Jesus Christ, Mary, the Sacraments, Celibacy, Women Religious, Evangelization, Catholic Education, Evil, Ecumenism, the Arts, and Easter.

These final selections, of course, do not encompass the vast scope of the Pope's knowledge and interests, not to mention his words in books, speeches, homilies, letters, and encyclicals on an extraordinarily wide range of matters both religious and secular. In his many years as Pope, he has adhered to a punishing schedule, both at the Vatican and abroad, on more than sixty trips, throughout all of which he has delivered as many as three memorable addresses a day, almost every day of the year. His collected speeches and addresses alone add up to some twenty volumes (most of which are available in the journal *The Pope Speaks*).

Moreover, before ascending to the Papacy, John Paul had been a poet, a playwright, and a drama critic, as well as a philosopher of distinction, none of which vocations has been represented in this collection because of constraints of space and the focus on popular themes and vital questions. Thus, these selections explore various key elements of Christian living and Catholic faith. But any reader can easily think of many more topics that could have been added.

CHRISTIAN LIFE

Jesus Christ

Christ is the one awaited by all peoples, He is God's answer to humanity. After the long period of "evangelical preparations"

(Eusebius of Caesarea), here He comes from the Father's bosom. He comes to be a man like us, to offer God the supreme act of worship and love which alone could reconcile Him with man.

THE CHURCH IN THE WORLD OF THE 1980S
Address to Cardinals, Rome, December 22, 1980

We are living in an era of great changes: the rapid decline of ideologies that seemed to promise a long resistance to the wear and tear of time; the racing out on the planet of new confines and frontiers. Humanity often finds itself uncertain, bewildered and anxious (cf. Mt 24:35). The faith of the Church is founded on Jesus Christ, the one Savior of the world, yesterday and today and forever (cf. Heb 13:8). It gives Christ reference for the answer to the question rising up from the human heart in the face of the mystery of life and death. Only from Christ, indeed, can there be answers that do not deceive nor disappoint. . . . Jesus dwells among those who call on Him without having known Him; among those who, after beginning to know Him, have lost Him through no fault of their own; among those who seek Him in sincerity of heart, while coming from different cultural and religious contexts.

ADDRESS TO YOUNG PEOPLE FOR THE TWELFTH WORLD YOUTH
DAY, August 15, 1996

Jesus is the Son of God "incarnate," come in the flesh, in order to live the concrete realities of our existence as man and as the Son of God at the same time. It is an unprecedented mystery. You have an inkling of the dignity that He conferred on your lives as humble workers, since he lived in Nazareth, in Palestine. He lived it under the gaze of God His Father, intimately linked to Him in the action of grace. He offered to God all its joys and all its difficulties. He lived it with simplicity, purity of heart, with courage, as a servant, as a friend welcoming the sick, the afflicted, the poor of every kind, with a love that no one will surpass and which He made His testament: Love one another, as I have loved you. It is that life which, through the trial of His sacrifice offered to free the world from its sins, is now glorified before God.

HOMILY AT KISANGANI, ZAIRE, May 29, 1980

We cannot learn Christianity as a lesson made up of various chapters, but it is always linked with a person, a living person, Jesus Christ. Jesus Christ is both guide and model. It is possible to imitate Him in different ways and in varying degrees to make Him the "rule" of one's own life.

ADDRESS TO YOUTH AT PARIS, June 1, 1980

The Church has always taught and continues to proclaim that God's revelation was brought to completion in Jesus Christ, who is the fullness of that revelation, and that "no new public revelation is to be expected before the glorious manifestation of Our Lord" (Constitution on Divine Revelation, 4). The Church evaluates and judges private revelations by the criterion of conformity with that single public revelation.

THE MESSAGE OF FATIMA, May 13, 1982

Mary

Consecrating the world to the immaculate heart of Mary means drawing near, through the Mother's intercession, to the very fountain of life that sprang from Golgotha. This fountain unceasingly pours forth redemption and grace. In it reparation is made continually for the sins of the world. It is a ceaseless source of new life and holiness.

THE MESSAGE OF FATIMA, May 13, 1982

As we have seen, the Gospels contain the explicit affirmation for a virginal conception of the biological order, brought about by the Holy Spirit. The Church made this truth her own, beginning with the very first formulations of the faith.

CATECHESIS NO. 26 IN THE SERIES ON THE BLESSED VIRGIN
MARY, July 10, 1996

Mary lived and exercised her freedom precisely by giving herself to God and accepting God's gift within herself. Until the time of His birth, she sheltered in her womb the Son of God who became man; she raised Him and enabled Him to grow, and she accompanied Him in that supreme act of freedom which is the complete sacrifice of His own life. By the gift of herself, Mary entered fully into the plan of God who gives Himself to the world. By accepting and pondering in her heart events which she did not always understand (cf. Lk 2:19), she became the model of all those who hear the word of God and keep it (cf. Lk 11:28), and merited the title of seat of wisdom. This wisdom is Jesus Christ Himself, the eternal Word of God, who perfectly reveals and accomplishes the will of the Father (cf. Heb 10:5–10). To us too she addresses the command she gave to the servants at Cana in Galilee during the marriage feast: "Do whatever he tells you" (Jn 2:5).

ENCYCLICAL: THE SPLENDOR OF TRUTH (*Veritatis Splendor*), 1993

Motherhood means caring for the life of the child. Since Mary is the mother of us all, her care for the life of man is universal. The care of a mother embraces her child totally. Mary's motherhood has its beginning in her motherly care for Christ. In Christ, at the foot of the cross, she accepted John, and in John she accepted all of us totally.

THE MESSAGE OF FATIMA, May 13, 1982

The Sacraments

The Eucharist is also a great call to conversion. We know that it is an invitation to the banquet; that, by nourishing ourselves on the Eucharist, we receive in it the body and blood of Christ, under the appearances of bread and wine. Precisely because of this invitation, the Eucharist is and remains the call to conversion. If we receive it as such a call, such an invitation, it brings forth in us its proper fruits. It transforms our lives. It makes us a "new man," a "new creature" (cf. Gal 6:15; Eph 2:15; 2 Cor 5:17). It helps us not to be "overcome by evil, but to overcome evil by good" (cf. Rom 12:21). The Eucharist helps love to triumph in us—love over hatred, zeal over indifference.

HOMILY IN DUBLIN'S PHOENIX PARK, September 29, 1979

Though they differ from one another in essence and not only in degree, the common priesthood of the faithful and the ministerial or hierarchical priesthood are nonetheless interrelated. Each of them in its own special way is a participation in the one priesthood of Christ. The ministerial priest, by the sacred power he enjoys, molds and rules the priestly people. Acting in the person of Christ, he brings about the Eucharistic Sacrifice, and offers it to God in the name of all the people. For their part, the faithful join in the offering of the Eucharist by virtue of their royal priesthood. They likewise exercise that priesthood by receiving the sacraments, by prayer and thanksgiving, by the witness of a holy life, and by self-denial and active charity.

LETTER ON THE FIFTIETH ANNIVERSARY OF HIS PRIESTLY
ORDINATION, March 17, 1996

The confessional is not and cannot be an alternative to the psychoanalyst's or psychotherapist's office, nor can one expect the Sacrament of Penance to heal truly pathological conditions. The confessor is not a physician or a healer in the technical sense of the term; in fact, if the condition of the penitent seems to require medical care, the confessor should not deal with the matter himself, but should send the penitent to competent and honest professionals.

MESSAGE TO CARDINAL WILLIAM W. BAUM, MAJOR
PENITENTIARY, March 20, 1998

From the Eucharist springs the Church's mission and capacity to offer her specific contribution to the human family.

The Eucharist effectively transmits Christ's parting gift to the world: "Peace I give you, my peace I leave you" (cf. Jn 14:27).

The Eucharist is the sacrament of Christ's "peace" because it is the memorial of the salvific redemptive sacrifice of the cross.

The Eucharist is the sacrament of victory over the divisions that flow from personal sin and collective selfishness.

Therefore, the Eucharistic community is called to be a model and instrument of a reconciled humanity.

In the Christian community there can be no division, no discrimination, no separation among those who break the bread of life around the one altar of sacrifice.

HOMILY AT SEOUL, SOUTH KOREA, October 18, 1988

Baptism is the first and fundamental consecration of the human person. Beginning new existence in Christ, the baptized—man or woman—participates in this consecration, in this total donation to the Father which is proper to His eternal Son. It is He Himself—the Son—who incites in man's soul the desire to give oneself without reservation to God: "My soul thirsts for God, for the living God. When shall I come and behold the face of God?" (Ps 42:3).

WHAT WOULD THE WORLD BE WITHOUT CONSECRATED LIFE?
Homily at Mass, 1994 Synod of Bishops, October 29, 1994

The apostle Paul said: "God . . . has entrusted to us the ministry of reconciliation" (2 Cor 5:18). The people of God are called to a continual conversion, to an ever renewed reconciliation with God in Christ. This reconciliation is effected in the Sacrament of Penance, and it is there that you exercise, par excellence, your ministry of reconciliation.

ADDRESS TO THE PRIESTS OF ZAIRE, May 4, 1980

Celibacy

Priests in the Latin Church take on the commitment to live in celibacy. If vocation is watchfulness, certainly a significant aspect of the latter is fidelity to this commitment throughout one's whole life. But celibacy is only one of the dimensions of a vocation—a vocation which is lived out, along the journey of life, as part of an overall commitment to the many different tasks which derive from the priesthood.

LETTER ON THE FIFTIETH ANNIVERSARY OF HIS PRIESTLY
ORDINATION, March 17, 1996

The priest who, in the choice of celibacy, renounces human love to be opened totally to that of God, makes himself free to be given to men by a gift excluding no one, but including them all in the flow of charity which comes from God (cf. Rom 5:5) and leads to God. Celibacy, in linking the priest to God, frees him for all the works required by the care of souls.

ADDRESS TO THE PRIESTS OF ZAIRE, May 4, 1980

In the light of this principle so many other aspects of the priesthood are clarified: The value of celibacy is proclaimed, not so much as a practical exigency, but as an expression of a perfect offering and of a configuration to Jesus Christ.

Ad Limina ADDRESS TO U.S. BISHOPS, September 9, 1983

Women Religious

Since the beginning of my pontificate I have striven to point out the importance of religious consecration in the Church and the value of religious life as it affects the whole community of the faithful. Religious have the task of showing forth the holiness of the whole body of Christ and of bearing witness to a new and eternal life acquired by the redemption of Christ (cf. *Lumen Gentium,* n. 44). At the same time they are called to many different apostolates in the Church. Their service in the Gospel is very necessary for the life of the Church.

ADDRESS TO BISHOPS AT NAIROBI, KENYA, May 29, 1980

Your mission might appear to you to be too demanding, too big for your capabilities. For you are near the people; in many cases you have the education of children in your hands, the education of young people and adults. By nature and your evangelical mission you have to be sowers of peace and concord, unity and fraternity. You can disconnect the mechanisms of violence through integral education and promoting the authentic values of the person. Your consecrated lives have to be a challenge to egoism and oppression, a call to conversion, a factor of reconciliation among people.

ADDRESS TO WOMEN RELIGIOUS IN COSTA RICA, March 3, 1983

To women religious is due a very special debt of gratitude for their particular contribution to the field of education. Their authentic educational apostolate was, and is, worthy of the greatest praise. It is an apostolate that requires much self-sacrifice; it is thoroughly human as an expression of religious service; an apostolate that follows closely human and spiritual growth, and accompanies children and young people patiently and lovingly through the problems of youth and the insecurity of adolescence toward Christian maturity.

ADDRESS TO U.S. BISHOPS, October 28, 1993

Your consecration binds you to the Church in a special way (cf. *Lumen Gentium,* 44); in perfect communion with her, with her mission, with her pastors and with her faithful, you will find the full meaning of your religious life. Go on being, as consecrated women, the honor of mother Church.

ADDRESS TO WOMEN RELIGIOUS IN COSTA RICA, March 3, 1983

Precisely this femininity—often considered by a certain public opinion as foolishly sacrificed in religious life—is in fact rediscovered and expanded to a superior level: that of the kingdom of God.

ADDRESS TO WOMEN RELIGIOUS IN ZAIRE, May 3, 1980

Evangelization

The task of evangelization equally concerns all Christians—Catholic, Orthodox and Protestant. We must present to the world a unanimous witness to Jesus Christ, Son of the living God, who rose from the dead and revealed the face of the one God to all men. All Christians are called to carry out this mission according to their vocation. The task of evangelization involves moving towards each other and moving together as Christians, and it must begin from within; evangelization and unity, evangelization and ecumenism are indissolubly linked with each other.

ADDRESS AT AN ECUMENICAL LITURGY OF THE WORD IN GERMANY, June 22, 1996

In this time of grace for the whole Church, Chinese Catholics too must feel deeply committed to the new evangelization and to the preaching of the Gospel *ad gentes.* Both aspects of the Church's missionary mandate are essential to authentic ecclesial renewal. Asia is waiting to hear the word of God, and it must be above all Asians themselves who ensure that it takes deep root in the continent's ancient cultures. In your case, the inculturation of the Gospel in your own culture must show that there can be no opposition or incompatibility between being at one and the same time truly Catholic and truly Chinese.

ADDRESS TO CHINESE BISHOPS, August 19, 1995

With regard then to the relationship between missionary activity and the colonizing policies of some countries, it is necessary calmly and clearly to analyze the facts which show that if in some cases the coincidence had led to reprehensible behavior on the part of missionaries in relation to their countries of origin or in collaboration with local authorities whom it was not always possible to ignore, nevertheless, considered overall, evangelizing activity has always been distinguished by a very different goal from that of earthly powers: to promote the personal dignity of the evangelized, giving them access to the divine sonship obtained for every man by Christ and communicated to the faithful in baptism. In fact, this generally encouraged the progress of those peoples towards their freedom and development even at the social and economic level.

ADDRESS ON THE MYSTERY OF THE CHURCH, May 3, 1995

We must also be deeply convinced of the fact that evangelization is also a valuable service to humanity, since it prepares it to achieve the plan of God, who wishes to unite to Himself all men and women and render them a people of brothers and sisters liberated from injustices and filled with feelings of authentic solidarity.

MESSAGE FOR WORLD MISSION DAY, October 22, 2000

Catholic Education

The first principle of the Church's social teaching, from which all others derive: the center of the social order is man, considered in his inalienable dignity as a creature made "in the image of God." The value of society comes from the value of man, and not vice versa.

WHAT CHURCH TEACHING IS AND IS NOT, September 9, 1993

Having become almost universal, sport undoubtedly has its place in the Christian vision of culture and can promote both physical health and interpersonal relationships. However, sport can be taken over by commercial interests or become a vehicle for expressing tribal, national or racial rivalries, and give rise to occasional violence. . . . So it is an important area for a modern pastoral approach.

TOWARDS A PASTORAL APPROACH TO CULTURE
Document of the Pontifical Council for Culture, May 23, 1999

More than ever, the Church must make its own the words of the apostle: "I am ruined if I do not preach the gospel!" (1 Cor 9:16).

ADDRESS ON WORLD MISSION DAY, October 18, 1981

Educators, you have been confided the responsibility to guide the young generations toward an authentic culture of love, offering yourselves as tutor and model of faithfulness to the ideal values which give meaning to life.

ADDRESS AT THE VATICAN AIDS CONFERENCE, November 15, 1989

In the history of your country, an extremely effective instrument of Catholic education has been the Catholic school. It has contributed immensely to the spreading of God's word and has enabled the faithful "to relate human affairs and activities with religious values in a single living synthesis" (*Sapientia Christiana,* 1). In the community formed by the Catholic school, the power of the Gospel has been brought to bear on thought patterns, standards of judgment and norms of behavior.

ADDRESS TO U.S. BISHOPS, November 17, 1983

Historically, the Church was the founder of universities. For centuries it developed there a conception of the world in which the knowledge of the epoch was situated within the more ample vision of a world created by God and redeemed by our Lord Jesus Christ. Thus, many of its sons consecrated themselves to teaching and research to initiate generations of students into the various degrees of scholarship within a total vision of man, including especially a consideration of the ultimate reasons for his existence.

ADDRESS TO ZAIREAN STUDENTS, May 29, 1980

As an institution the Catholic school has to be judged extremely favorably if we apply the sound criterion "You will know them by their deeds" (Mt 7:16, and again, "You can tell a tree by its fruit"

(Mt 7:20). It is easy therefore in the cultural environment of the
United States to explain the wise exhortation contained in the
new code: "The faithful are to promote Catholic schools, doing
everything possible to help in establishing and maintaining them"
(Can 800:2).

ADDRESS TO U.S. BISHOPS, November 17, 1983

Catholic education in your land has also fostered numerous vocations over the years. You yourselves owe a great debt of gratitude
to that Catholic education which enabled you to understand and
to accept the call of the Lord. Among other contributions of
Catholic education is the quality of citizens that you were able to
produce: upright men and women who contributed to the well-
being of America, and through Christian charity worked to serve
all their brothers and sisters. Catholic education has furnished an
excellent witness to the Church's perennial commitment to culture of every kind. It has exercised a prophetic role—perhaps
modestly in individual cases, but overall most effectively—to
assist faith to permeate culture. The achievements of Catholic
education in America merit our great respect and admiration.

ADDRESS TO U.S. BISHOPS, November 17, 1983

There is still, however, a debt of gratitude to be paid, before the
witness of history, to the parents who have supported a whole system of Catholic education; to the parishes that have coordinated
and sustained these efforts; to the dioceses that have promoted
programs of education and supplemented means of support,
especially in poor areas; to the teachers—who always included a
certain number of generous lay men and women—who through
dedication and sacrifice championed the cause of helping young
people to reach maturity in Christ.

ADDRESS TO U.S. BISHOPS, November 17, 1983

The catechism is truly God's timely gift to the whole Church and
to every Christian at the approach of the new millennium.
Indeed, I pray that the Church in the United States will recognize
in the catechism an authoritative guide to sound and vibrant
preaching, an invaluable resource for parish adult formation pro-

grams, a basic text for the upper grades of Catholic high schools, colleges and universities. The catechism presents in a clear and complete way the riches of the Church's sacramental doctrine based on its genuine sources: Sacred Scripture and tradition as witnessed to by the fathers, doctors and saints, and by the constant teaching of the magisterium.

Ad Limina ADDRESS TO BISHOPS FROM ALABAMA, KENTUCKY, LOUISIANA, MISSISSIPPI, AND TENNESSEE, June 5, 1993

Evil

Redemption is always greater than man's sin and the "sin of the world." The power of the Redemption is infinitely superior to the whole range of evil in man and the world.

THE MESSAGE OF FATIMA, May 13, 1982

The contraposition of good and evil entered the history of man, destroying the original innocence in the heart of man and woman. "Although set by God in a state of rectitude, man, enticed by the evil one, abused his freedom at the very start of history. He lifted himself up against God and sought to attain his goal apart from him." From then, "the whole life of men, both individual and social, shows itself to be a struggle, and a dramatic one, between good and evil, between light and darkness. . . . For sin brought man to a lower state, forcing him away from the completeness that is his to attain" (*Gaudium et Spes,* 13).

HOMILY AT THE OPENING MASS OF THE SYNOD OF BISHOPS, September 29, 1983

Ecumenism

True peace can exist only on the basis of a process of unification in which each people is able to choose, in freedom and truth, the paths of its own development. Moreover, such a process is impossible if there is no agreement on the original and fundamental unity which is manifested in different forms, not opposed but complementary, which need one another and seek one another.

APOSTOLIC LETTER ON THE MILLENNIUM OF THE BAPTISM OF KIEVAN RUSS, 1988

Between the Catholic Church and the other Christian Churches and ecclesial communities there exists a drive toward communion rooted in the baptism which each administers. It is a drive nourished by prayer, dialogue and joint action.

ECCLESIA IN AMERICA
Post-synodal Apostolic Exhortation, January 22, 1999

Thus it is absolutely clear that ecumenism, the movement promoting Christian unity, is not just some sort of appendix which is added to the Church's traditional activity. Rather, ecumenism is an organic part of her life and work, and consequently must pervade all that she is and does. It must be like the fruit borne by a healthy and flourishing tree which grows to its full stature.

ENCYCLICAL: THAT ALL MAY BE ONE (*Unum Sint*), 1995

We look forward to the celebration of two thousand years since the Word became flesh and dwelt among us (cf. Jn 1:14). This is an opportunity to proclaim afresh our common faith in God who loved the world so much that He sent His Son, not to condemn the world but so that the world might be saved through Him (cf. Jn 3:16–17). We encourage Anglicans and Catholics, with all their Christian brothers and sisters, to pray, celebrate and witness together in the Year 2000. We make this call in a spirit of humility, recognizing that credible witness will only be fully given when Anglicans and Catholics, with all their Christian brothers and sisters, have achieved that full, visible unity that corresponds to Christ's prayer "that they may all be one . . . so that the world may believe" (Jn 17:21).

JOINT DECLARATION OF POPE JOHN PAUL II AND ARCHBISHOP
GEORGE CAREY OF CANTERBURY, December 5, 1996

In view of all this, the Catholic Church desires nothing less than full communion between East and West. She finds inspiration for this in the experience of the first millennium. . . . How can unity be restored after almost a thousand years? This is the great task which the Catholic Church must accomplish, a task equally incumbent on the Orthodox Church. Thus can be understood the continuing relevance of dialogue, guided by the light and strength of the Holy Spirit.

ENCYCLICAL: THAT ALL MAY BE ONE (*Unum Sint*), 1995

In these moments full of joy and after having the experience of a profound spiritual communion which we desire to share with the pastors and the faithful as much of the East as of the West, we lift up our hearts toward Him who is the head, Christ. It is from Him that the entire body receives concord and cohesion thanks to all the members who serve it by an activity shared according to the capacity of each. Thus the body realizes its natural growth. Thus, the body constructs itself in love (cf. Eph 4:16).

JOINT DECLARATION OF POPE JOHN PAUL II AND PATRIARCH DIMITRIOS I, December 7, 1987

The churches of the East and the West, over the centuries, have celebrated together the ecumenical councils which have proclaimed and defended "the faith which was once for all handed down to the holy ones" (Jude 3). "Called to the one hope" (Eph 4:4), we wait for the day desired by God when the rediscovered unity in the faith will be celebrated and when full communion will be reestablished by a concelebration of the Eucharist of the Lord.

JOINT DECLARATION OF POPE JOHN PAUL II AND PATRIARCH DIMITRIOS I, December 7, 1987

The Arts

Every piece of art, be it religious or secular, be it a painting, a sculpture, a poem or any form of handicraft made by loving skill, is a sign and a symbol of the inscrutable secret of human existence, of man's origin and destiny, of the meaning of his life and work. It speaks to us of the meaning of birth and death, of the greatness of man.

ADDRESS AT CLONMACNOISE, IRELAND, September 30, 1979

For a long time, the Church was considered the mother of the arts. It was the Church which commissioned art. The contents of Christian faith determined the motifs and themes of art. How true this is can easily be demonstrated by stopping to think what would remain if one removed everything connected with religious and Christian inspiration from European and German art history. In recent centuries, most strongly since about 1800, the connection between the Church and culture, and thus between the Church and art, has grown more tenuous.

ADDRESS AT MUNICH, November 19, 1980

Today, literature, the theater, film and the visual arts see their function largely in terms of criticism, protest, opposition and pointing an accusing finger at existing conditions. The beautiful as a category of art seems to have fallen by the wayside in favor of depictions of man in his negative aspects, in his contradictions, in his hopelessness and in the absence of meaning. This seems to be the current *ecce homo*. The so-called intact world is an object of scorn and cynicism.

ADDRESS AT MUNICH, November 19, 1980

Easter

This is the day that the Lord has made for us. The day of a great testimony and a great challenge. The day of God's great response to man's unceasing questions. Questions about man, his origin and his destiny, about the meaning and dimension of his existence. This is the day the Lord has made for us. "Christ, our Paschal lamb, has been sacrificed" (1 Cor 5:7). "Pasch" means passing. The passing of God through human history. Passing through the inevitability of human death, which from the beginning and until the end is the gate to eternity. Passing through the history of human sin, which in God's heart is man's death: passing to life in God.

EASTER MESSAGE, March 30, 1986

"This is the day that the Lord has made" (Ps 118:24). This day ever reconfirms this truth for us: God does not "resign" Himself to man's death. Christ came into the world to convince it of this. Christ died on the cross and was placed in the tomb to bear witness precisely to this fact: God does not "resign" Himself to man's death. For He "is not God of the dead, but of the living" (Mt 22:32). In Christ death has been defied. Christ by His death has conquered death. Behold the day which the Lord has made. This is the day of God's great uprising: His uprising against death.

The last word of God on the human condition is not death but life; not despair but hope. To this hope the Church invites the men and women of today as well. She repeats to them the incredible but true proclamation: Christ is risen! Let the whole world rise with Him! Alleluia!

EASTER MESSAGE, March 30, 1986

CHRONOLOGY OF THE LIFE
OF KAROL JÓZEF WOJTYLA,
POPE JOHN PAUL II

JULY 18, 1879. Karol's father, Karol Wojtyla, son of a master tailor, is born in Lipnik, Poland.

MARCH 26, 1884. Karol's mother, Emilia Kaczorowska, daughter of a saddle maker, is born in Kraków.

AUGUST 27, 1906. Karol's brother, Edmund, is born.

MAY 18, 1920. Karol Józef Wojtyla is born in Wadowice and baptized on June 20.

SEPTEMBER 15, 1926. Karol begins elementary school.

APRIL 13, 1929. Karol's mother dies.

DECEMBER 5, 1932. Karol's brother, Edmund, a physician, dies.

FALL 1934. Karol begins performing in plays.

MAY 3, 1938. Karol is confirmed.

MAY 27, 1938. Karol is named class valedictorian and graduates from high school.

SUMMER 1938. Karol joins the "Studio 38" experimental theater group founded by Tadeusz Kudlinski.

AUGUST 1938. Karol begins studies at Jagiellonian University in Kraków.

JULY 1939. Karol completes military training with the Academic Legion.

NOVEMBER 1939. Nearly two hundred professors from his university are arrested and deported to a concentration camp. Karol begins clandestine studies and underground cultural activities.

SPRING–SUMMER 1940. Karol writes two plays, *Job: A Drama from the Old Testament* and *Jeremiah: A National Drama in Three Acts.*

FEBRUARY 18, 1941. Karol's father, a retired Polish army officer, dies.

FALL 1942. Karol begins underground studies as a seminarian with the Archdiocese of Kraków.

JANUARY 1945. The Nazis leave Kraków, and the Red Army takes over.

NOVEMBER 1, 1946. Karol is ordained a priest.

NOVEMBER 1946–JUNE 1948. Wojtyla pursues graduate studies in Rome and is awarded his first doctorate.

JULY 28, 1948. Wojtyla is given his first assignment as a parish priest in Niegowic, Poland.

1949–1950. Wojtyla publishes a play, *Our God's Brother,* and a cycle of poems, "Song of the Brightness of Water."

AUGUST 1950. Wojtyla is recalled to Kraków to be assistant pastor at St. Florian's.

JANUARY 1954. Wojtyla earns a second doctorate in theology from Jagiellonian University.

DECEMBER 1, 1956. Wojtyla is appointed to the Chair of Ethics at the Catholic University of Lublin.

1957–1958. Wojtyla publishes two more poem cycles, "Profiles of a Cyrenean" and "The Quarry," both pseudonymously.

JULY 4, 1958. Wojtyla is named Auxiliary Bishop of Kraków by Pope Pius XII.

JANUARY 1960. Wojtyla's book *Love and Responsibility* is published.

DECEMBER 1960. Wojtyla's play *The Jeweler's Shop* is published.

OCTOBER 11, 1962. Vatican II opens.

NOVEMBER 1962. Wojtyla speaks to the Council on liturgical reform and speaks during the Council debate on revelation.

DECEMBER 30, 1962. Wojtyla is designated Metropolitan Bishop of Kraków.

NOVEMBER 1963. Wojtyla's poem cycle on Vatican II, "The Church," is published pseudonymously.

DECEMBER 30, 1963. Pope Paul VI names Wojtyla Archbishop of Kraków.

SEPTEMBER 25, 1964. Wojtyla addresses Vatican II on religious freedom.

JUNE 1965. Wojtyla publishes the poem cycle "Holy Places" pseudonymously.

SEPTEMBER 28, 1965. Wojtyla speaks at Vatican II on modern atheism.

JUNE 28, 1967. Pope Paul VI makes Wojtyla a Cardinal.

FALL 1969. Wojtyla travels through Canada and the United States, establishes the archdiocesan Institute of Family Studies, and takes part in the international Synod of Bishops in Rome.

1969. Wojtyla publishes a major work of philosophy, *Person and Act.*

1970. Wojtyla publishes "Sources of Renewal," a guide to the documents of Vatican II.

FEBRUARY 1973. Wojtyla represents the Polish Church at the International Eucharistic Congress in Melbourne.

APRIL 16, 1974. Wojtyla speaks at the funeral of Cardinal Stefan Trochta, defying the Polish Communist regime.

MAY 1975. Wojtyla publishes the poem cycle "Meditation on Death" pseudonymously.

SUMMER 1976. Wojtyla attends the International Eucharistic Congress in Philadelphia.

AUGUST 6, 1978. Paul VI dies.

AUGUST 25, 1978. Albino Luciani is selected Pope and becomes John Paul I. He dies on September 29.

OCTOBER 16, 1978. Wojtyla is elected Pope and becomes John Paul II.

DECEMBER 11, 1978. John Paul II speaks on religious freedom on the thirtieth anniversary of the Universal Declaration of Human Rights.

MARCH 4, 1979. John Paul II's first encyclical, *Redemptor Hominis,* is published.

JUNE 2–10, 1979. John Paul II visits Poland for the first time as Pope.

SEPTEMBER 29–OCTOBER 1, 1979. John Paul II makes his first papal pilgrimage to Ireland.

OCTOBER 1–7, 1979. John Paul II makes his first pilgrimage to the United States, where he addresses the United Nations.

AUGUST 1980. The Solidarity trade union movement is born in Gdansk. John Paul II writes to Polish Church leaders supporting strikers' demands.

DECEMBER 1980. John Paul II writes to Leonid Brezhnev in support of Polish sovereignty.

JANUARY 15, 1981. John Paul II receives a Solidarity delegation at the Vatican.

MAY 13, 1981. John Paul II is shot by Mehmet Alì Agca in St. Peter's Square.

DECEMBER 1981. General Jaruzelski imposes martial law in Poland and begins mass arrests of Solidarity members. John Paul II urges Jaruzelski to end the violence.

JANUARY 1, 1982. John Paul II denounces the "false peace" of totalitarian states in a message on the World Day of Peace.

JUNE 7, 1982. John Paul II meets with Ronald Reagan at the Vatican.

JUNE 1983. John Paul II makes his second pilgrimage to Poland.

JULY 1983. General Jaruzelski lifts martial law in Poland.

OCTOBER 1983. Lech Walesa wins the Nobel Peace Prize.

NOVEMBER 1983. John Paul II writes to Deng Xiaoping requesting direct contacts with the government of China.

JANUARY 1984. Full diplomatic relations between the United States and the Vatican are established.

JUNE 24, 1985. The Commission for Religious Relations with the Jews issues *Notes on the Correct Way to Present the Jews and Judaism in Preaching and Catechesis in the Roman Catholic Church*.

AUGUST 19, 1985. John Paul II addresses a large audience of Muslims in Casablanca.

APRIL 13, 1986. John Paul II appears at the Synagogue of Rome to address the Roman Jewish community.

FALL 1986. John Paul II travels to Bangladesh, Singapore, Fiji, New Zealand, Australia, and the Seychelles.

SEPTEMBER 10–21, 1987. John Paul II makes his second pilgrimage to the United States.

JUNE 7, 1988. John Paul II writes to Mikhail Gorbachev, opening conversations with the Soviet leader.

AUGUST 15, 1988. John Paul II's apostolic letter on the dignity of women (*Mulieris Dignitatem*) is published.

WINTER–SPRING 1989. Solidarity sweeps elections in Poland.

SEPTEMBER 12, 1989. The first postwar non-Communist leader of Poland, Tadeusz Masowiecki, takes office.

DECEMBER 1, 1989. Mikhail Gorbachev visits John Paul II at the Vatican.

MARCH 1, 1990. The Vatican establishes diplomatic relations with the USSR.

JANUARY 15, 1991. John Paul II urges, in letters to George Bush and Saddam Hussein, a negotiated end to the crisis in the Persian Gulf.

JULY 15, 1992. John Paul II undergoes surgery for removal of a benign intestinal tumor.

OCTOBER 31, 1992. John Paul II, receiving the report of a papal commission on Galileo, urges a dialogue between science and religion.

DECEMBER 5, 1992. John Paul II asserts that there is a duty to intervene in cases of possible genocide.

APRIL 9, 1993. John Paul II writes to Carmelite nuns in their convent near Auschwitz, advising them to find another location for their work.

SEPTEMBER 1993. John Paul II makes a pilgrimage to Lithuania, Latvia, and Estonia.

NOVEMBER 11, 1993. John Paul II breaks his shoulder.

MARCH 25, 1994. John Paul II's eleventh encyclical, *Evangelium Vitae,* is published.

APRIL 7, 1994. John Paul II attends the Holocaust Memorial Concert in Rome.

APRIL 28, 1994. John Paul II fractures his leg and has his hip replacement surgery.

SEPTEMBER 29, 1994. Israel's first ambassador to the Vatican presents his credentials to John Paul II.

OCTOBER 19, 1994. John Paul II's book *Crossing the Threshold of Hope* is published.

OCTOBER 25, 1994. The Palestine Liberation Organization and the Vatican establish official relations.

JANUARY–DECEMBER 1995. John Paul II issues repeated appeals for peace in the Balkans.

JANUARY 15, 1995. John Paul II says Mass before a huge crowd in Manila at the fifth international World Youth Day.

SEPTEMBER 4–15, 1995. The Fourth World Conference on Women meets in Beijing.

OCTOBER 5, 1995. John Paul II addresses the fiftieth meeting of the UN General Assembly during his third pilgrimage to the United States.

MARCH 1996. John Paul II makes his first pilgrimage to reunified Germany.

OCTOBER 8, 1996. John Paul II has an appendectomy.

NOVEMBER 15, 1996. John Paul II's memoir *Gift and Mystery* is published.

DECEMBER 1996. George Carey, Archbishop of Canterbury, visits Rome.

SEPTEMBER 5, 1997. Mother Teresa dies in Calcutta.

JANUARY 1998. John Paul II makes his first pilgrimage to Cuba.

MARCH 16, 1998. The Commission for Religious Relations with the Jews publishes "We Remember: A Reflection on the Shoah."

OCTOBER 18, 1998. John Paul II celebrates the twentieth anniversary of his Papacy with a Mass in St. Peter's Square.

APRIL 4, 1999. John Paul II renews his appeal for peace in Kosovo in his Easter Message "Urbi et Orbi."

APRIL 26, 1999. John Paul II receives the Minister of Foreign Affairs of Israel, Ariel Sharon.

OCTOBER 31, 1999. The Catholic Church and the World Lutheran Federation sign the Joint Declaration on the Doctrine of Justification.

DECEMBER 24, 1999. The Great Jubilee of the Year 2000 begins. John Paul II opens the Holy Door of St. Peter's Basilica.

FEBRUARY 15, 2000. John Paul II receives Yasir Arafat, president of the Palestinian Authority, and signs a basic agreement between the Holy See and the Palestine Liberation Organization.

MARCH 20–26, 2000. John Paul II makes a Jubilee pilgrimage to Jordan, the Autonomous Territories of the Palestinian National Authority, and Israel.

JUNE 13, 2000. John Paul II expresses his satisfaction with the clemency granted to Alì Agca by the president of Italy.

SEPTEMBER 3, 2000. Pope Pius IX and Pope John XXIII are beatified.

OCTOBER 17, 2000. Queen Elizabeth II and Prince Philip make an official visit to the Vatican.

BIBLIOGRAPHY

The following bibliography is by no means complete or systematic, but it provides the reader with readily available English renderings in book form of the encyclicals, many important apostolic letters and apostolic exhortations, plus hundreds of speeches, sermons, and addresses. We have also included English translations of the Pope's poetry and dramatic works. Almost all of the Pope's speeches are published in periodicals, especially in the Vatican's *Osservatore Romano,* a weekly edition of which is published in English (as well as in many other languages), and in *The Pope Speaks,* a bimonthly magazine published by Our Sunday Visitor, Inc.

Apostolic Letter of His Holiness Pope John Paul II on the Christian Meaning of Human Suffering (St. Paul Editions, Boston, 1984)

Be Not Afraid: John Paul II Speaks Out on His Life, His Beliefs, and His Inspiring Vision for Humanity (St. Martin's Press, New York, 1984)

Blessed Are the Pure of Heart: Catechesis on the Sermon on the Mount and the Writings of St. Paul (St. Paul Editions, Boston, 1983)

Brazil: Journey in the Light of the Eucharist: Sermons (St. Paul Editions, Boston, 1980)

The Collected Plays and Writings on Theater (University of California Press, Berkeley, 1987)

Covenant of Love: Pope John Paul II on Sexuality, Marriage, and Family in the Modern World (Doubleday, Garden City, NY, 1985)

Crossing the Threshold of Hope (Alfred A. Knopf, New York, 1994)

Draw Near to God (Servant Books, Ann Arbor, MI, 1987)

Encyclical Letter Dives in Misericordia *of the Supreme Pontiff John Paul II on the Mercy of God* (St. Paul Editions, Boston, 1981)

The Encyclicals of John Paul II, edited with introductions by J. Michael Miller, CSB (Our Sunday Visitor Publishing Division, Huntington, IN, 1996)

Essays on Religious Freedom (Catholic League for Religious and Civil Rights, Milwaukee, 1984)

The Family: Center of Love and Life, compiled and indexed by the Daughters of St. Paul (St. Paul Editions, Boston, 1981)

The Far East Journey of Peace and Brotherhood (St. Paul Editions, Boston, 1981)

France: Message of Peace, Trust, Love, and Faith (St. Paul Editions, Boston, 1980)

Fruitful and Responsible Love (Seabury Press, New York, 1979)

Germany: Pilgrimage of Unity and Peace (St. Paul Editions, Boston, 1981)

Gift and Mystery: On the Fiftieth Anniversary of My Priestly Ordination (Doubleday, New York, 1996)

God, Father and Creator: A Catechesis on the Creed, Vol. 1 (Pauline Books and Media, Boston, 1996)

The Gospel of Life, the Papal Encyclical Evangelium Vitae. In *Origins: CNS Documentary Service,* April 6, 1995

I Believe in Youth, Christ Believes in Youth: To the Young People of the World (St. Paul Editions, Boston, 1981)

Jesus, Son and Savior: A Catechesis on the Creed, Vol. 2 (Pauline Books and Media, Boston, 1996)

John Paul II for Peace in the Middle East (Libreria Editrice Vaticana, Vatican City, 1992)

Letter of the Supreme Pontiff, Pope John Paul II, to All the Bishops of the Church on the Mystery of the Eucharist (St. Paul Editions, Boston, 1980)

Lord and Giver of Life: Encyclical Letter Dominum et vivificantem *of the Supreme Pontiff John Paul II on the Holy Spirit in the Life of the Church and the World* (U.S. Catholic Conference, Washington, DC, 1986)

Love and Responsibility (Ignatius Press, San Francisco, 1993)

Marian Reflections: The Angelus Messages of Pope John Paul II (AMI Press, Washington, DC, 1990)

On Human Work, Encyclical Laborem Exercens (St. Paul Editions, Boston, 1981)

Original Unity of Man and Woman: Catechesis on the Book of Genesis (St. Paul Editions, Boston, 1981)

Person and Community: Selected Essays (P. Lang Publishers, New York, 1993)

Pilgrim to Poland: Sermons (St. Paul Editions, Boston, 1979)

Pilgrimage of Peace: The Collected Speeches of John Paul II in Ireland and the United States (Farrar, Straus & Giroux, New York, 1980)

The Place Within: The Poetry of Pope John Paul II (Random House, New York, 1994)

The Pope and Revolution: John Paul II Confronts Liberation Theology (Ethics and Public Policy Center, Washington, DC, 1982)

Pope John Paul II on Jews and Judaism: 1979–1986 (U.S. Catholic Conference, Washington, DC, 1987)

The Pope Speaks to the American Church: John Paul's Homilies, Speeches, and Letters to Catholics in the United States (Harper-Collins, San Francisco, 1992)

The Post-Synodal Apostolic Exhortations of John Paul II, edited with introduction by J. Michael Miller, CSB (Our Sunday Visitor Publishing Division, Huntington, IN, 1998)

Prayers and Devotions, edited by Peter Canisius Johannes Van Lierde (Viking, New York, 1994)

Prayers and Devotions from Pope John Paul II: Selected Passages from His Writings and Speeches Arranged for Every Day of the Year (Regnery Gateway, Chicago, 1984)

Reflections on Humanae Vitae: *Conjugal Morality and Spirituality* (St. Paul Editions, Boston, 1984)

Sacred in All Its Forms (St. Paul Editions, Boston, 1984)

Second Pastoral Visit of His Holiness Pope John Paul II to the United States of America (Catholic Book Publishing Co., New York, 1987)

Sign of Contradiction (Seabury Press, New York, 1979)

Sources of Renewal: The Implementation of the Second Vatican Council (Harper & Row, San Francisco, 1980)

The Spirit, Giver of Life and Love: A Catechesis on the Creed, Vol. 3 (Pauline Books and Media, Boston, 1996)

Spiritual Pilgrimage: Texts on Jews and Judaism, 1979–1995, edited by Eugene Fisher and Leon Klenicki (Crossroad, New York, 1995)

Talks of John Paul II, compiled by the Daughters of St. Paul (St. Paul Editions, Boston, 1979)

The Theology of Marriage and Celibacy (St. Paul Editions, Boston, 1986)

The Theology of the Body (Pauline Books and Media, Boston, 1997)

Through the Priestly Ministry, The Gift of Salvation: Messages of John Paul II to Bishops, Priests, and Deacons (St. Paul Editions, Boston, 1982)

Through the Year with Pope John Paul II: Readings for Every Day of the Year (Crossroad, New York, 1981)

To the U.S. Bishops at Their Ad Limina *Visits: April 15–December 3, 1983* (St. Paul Editions, Boston, 1981)

The Way to Christ: Spiritual Exercises (HarperCollins, New York, 1994)

The Word Made Flesh: The Meaning of the Christmas Season (HarperCollins, New York, 1994)

Religion/Spirituality

John Paul II, the 264th successor to Saint Peter, has been pope for over two decades. The leader of the world's Catholics, his influence has been felt by Christians and non-Christians alike—indeed even by nonbelievers. Presidents and peasants the world over have come under his influence. By far the most traveled pontiff in the modern history of the Church, he has delivered his speeches and homilies to audiences around the world in their native languages.

Contained in *The Wisdom of John Paul II* are essential excerpts from papal encyclicals, sermons, addresses, and other statements, both formal and occasional, from throughout His Holiness's papacy. They discuss matters of faith and matters of conscience, and range from the problems of Contemporary Spirituality and Morality to Progress in the Modern World and Human Rights—all informed by the profound wisdom and deep understanding of a man who has devoted his life to God and His people.

U.S. $12.00
Can. $18.00

Cover design: John Gall
Cover art: © Arturo Mari/L'Osservatore Romano
Photo Service

ISBN 0-375-72732-9

51200

9 780375 727320

www.vintagebooks.com